I0137029

METAPHYSICS FOR EVERYONE

Interviews with Bruno Bérard

⊕

METAPHYSICS
FOR EVERYONE

Interviews with Bruno Bérard

⊕

Bruno Bérard
Annie Cidéron

Angelico Press

First published
by Angelico Press 2024
© Bruno Bérard 2024

All rights reserved

No part of this book may be reproduced or transmitted,
in any form or by any means, without permission.

For information, address:
Angelico Press
169 Monitor St.
Brooklyn, NY 11222
angelicopress.com

979-8-89280-046-4 (pbk)
979-8-89280-047-1 (cloth)
979-8-89280-048-8 (ebook)

Cover design: Michael Schrauzer

Table of Contents

Preface 1

PART I
General Metaphysics

Chapter 1: Metaphysics and Science 5
Where does the word "metaphysics" come from?—What is a science?—The limits of science—What is being?—What about non-being?—The limits of metaphysics—The pitfalls of metaphysics

Chapter 2: Metaphysics and Religion 19

Is God really dead?—The languages of metaphysics and religion—Christian metaphysics

Chapter 3: Metaphysics and Mysticism 35

Rational metaphysics and mystical metaphysics—What can be said of the inexpressible?—Proofs of the existence of God—Experiences of God

Chapter 4: Metaphysics and Esotericism 53
Esotericism, a brief inventory—Esoteric or esotericism?—Esotericism and metaphysics

PART II
Personal Metaphysics

Chapter 5: Metaphysical Biography 63
Words and thought—The others, the alter egos—What professional life?—Four significant encounters—Initiation, initiation books

Chapter 6: An Adventure into Metaphysics 80
Introduction à une métaphysique des mystères chrétiens (2005)—*A*

Metaphysics of the Christian Mysteries (2018) — *Introduzione a una metafisica cristiana* (2021) — *Jean Borella, The Metaphysical Revolution* (2006) — *Introduction à la métaphysique. Les trois songes* (2008) — *Collective books* — *Metaphysics of paradox* (2019) — *Lacuria* (2020) — *Métaphysique de Sexe* (2022) — *La démocratie du future, le partage du pouvoir* [*The Democracy of the Future, Power Sharing*] (2022)

Chapter 7: Metaphysics and Metaphysicians 94
Metaphysics, material object and formal object—Some metaphysicians:—*Plato*—*Aristotle*—*St Thomas Aquinas*—*St Bonaventure*—*Descartes*—*Leibniz*—*René Guénon*—*Frithjof Schuon*—*Jean Borella*

PART III
Special Metaphysics

Chapter 8: Metaphysics of Believing 115
To believe or to know?—Knowledge or cognizance?—What we believe in: *Symbolic theology*—*Affirmative theology*—*Negative theology*—*Mystical theology*—What is it to believe?

Chapter 9: Metaphysics of Sex 124
Context of a metaphysics of sex—Sexuations, genders, sexuality, an inventory—Where does love stand in all of this?—Sexual techniques—Metaphysics of sex and the sexes

Chapter 10: Metaphysics and Matter 131
Matter: scientific understanding—Materia: philosophical understanding—Cosmic substance: a traditional understanding—Creation ex nihilo: Christian understanding—Metaphysical conclusions: *Cosmology, Matter*

Chapter 11: Metaphysics and the *Post-Mortem* State 139
From the origin of being—Beyond Being—The Christological hologram—The afterlife

Chapter 12: What is Metaphysics? 146
Metaphysics as epiphany of the spirit—Metaphysics as a universal and final arbiter—Metaphysics as theology—To believe is to die in advance

Appendix I: Analogy of the Divided Line 157
Appendix II: The Two Step "Cure" 158
Appendix III: Some Texts About Believing 159
From the Same Author 164
Index of Names 167

Preface

Three things led me to take on this project. First, there were those metaphysical questions everyone asks themselves, such as "what was there before?," "what will come next?" The second is the need for the widest possible audience to access the beautiful answers of human thoughts over 2,500 years, other than through specialist books which are not easily accessed. And the third will have been the opportunity to meet Bruno Bérard.

The fact that he accepted that this communication work be done in the form of interviews, questions and answers, exchanges, seemed to me to favor a simpler—but not simplistic—presentation of a certain number of metaphysical questions, especially those that are the most impactful.

These interviews were conducted for a few hours each week over the course of nearly a year, and the result presented here is a simple reformatting, in line with Bruno Bérard's thinking, of course. As he himself says, he does not have any special claim on the truth, but this approach to metaphysics will at least have the advantage of a personal presentation—authentic and sincere.

Of course, the contributions of many illustrious metaphysicians are not absent from the remarks made here, and in order to give credit where credit was due, it was necessary to mention them by name. So as to not unnecessarily encumber the presentation of these interviews, quotations are limited to the essentials, and most often the sources are simply indicated in parentheses at the end of the paragraph. Moreover, we have tried to avoid footnotes.

Finally, in order to situate things more readily in time, dates of birth and death of some philosophers, metaphysicians, and scientists have been added.

It is indeed the characteristic of an entry into philosophy, and *a fortiori* into metaphysics, to accent the personal as well. Thus, two interviews focus on the personal side, one on a "metaphysical biography" of Bruno Bérard, the other on his "adventure in metaphysics" through a review of his books.

Even though the door to such an adventure has been thrown open here, it is up to each person who wishes to enter "within," or rather to step outside and walk in the open air of metaphysics.

May these few pages shed light on these twin journeys.

Annie Cidéron

PART I

General Metaphysics

Chapter 1
Metaphysics and Science

This interview was the first we conducted; it was necessary to begin with the word itself, then to ask oneself if, and to what extent, metaphysics could be a science, that is to say, lead to effective knowledge.

Annie Cidéron (**AC**): Starting with the name, many of us have wondered just what it is. Could you say something about the term "metaphysics"?

Where does the word "metaphysics" come from?

Bruno Bérard (**BB**): The word is simply composed of "physics," the science of the natural phenomena of the world and of matter, and "meta," which makes it the science of what is beyond nature and matter. It has taken more than fifteen centuries to arrive at its current precise definition:

There are, originally, the fourteen books of *Metaphysics* by Aristotle, written in the fourth century BC, but where the word metaphysics is itself not found.

A first designation appears three centuries later from the hand of a publisher of Aristotle's complete works (Nicolaus of Damascus): *ta meta ta phusika*, in four words, and meaning "what comes" (or, more precisely, "the question that arises") once one has encountered the physical world.

Finally, "metaphysics," in a single word, appears in the fourth century AD, in a catalog of the work of

The Philosopher (probably carried out by Hesychius of Miletus).

In the Middle Ages, "metaphysics" still referred to the initial fourteen books of Aristotle, but since then this word has come to refer to the science of what is beyond the physical world.

AC: Is metaphysics a science?

What is a science?

BB: Metaphysics has in fact a double source: Plato, who established once and for all the possibility of a knowledge of immaterial, immutable, universal, and intelligible realities; and Aristotle, who established once and for all the rigor of scientific discourse (Borella, 1930–). Even if it took more than a millennium and a half to achieve what is now called metaphysics, the subject was already treated philosophically by Plato and defined scientifically in the books of Aristotle. Metaphysics is thus both philosophy *and* science.

All science is defined as "knowledge by causes." There are thus physical causes such as gravity, which causes what is thrown up in the air to fall, and chemical causes, which make it possible to manufacture steel (iron + carbon) or decompose water into hydrogen and oxygen. But there are also more radical causes, those that lie behind questions like "who am I?" or "why is there something rather than nothing?"—the first being rather eastern (inner world), the second more western (outer world).

AC: That's all well and good, but in one case we have ascertainable causes, while, in the case of metaphysics, hypothetical causes, right?

BB: Not quite! First of all, the various sciences deal with

successive causes: heat comes from combustion, which in turn needs oxygen produced by plants thanks to photosynthesis, due in turn to the sun and chlorophyll, etc. (Pamphile, 1925–2019). Therefore, it is up to the "science of sciences," metaphysics, to stop this indefinite merry-go-round of secondary causes. The Greeks already said: *ananké sténai*: "it is necessary to stop!" This sequence of second causes must lead to a first cause, what Aristotle called the "immobile mover." And the founder of science himself comes to this conclusion!

Next, the sciences are constituted within limits that define them: zoology, botany, history, mathematics, psychology, chemistry, computer science, pharmacology, etc. Therefore, they cannot and must not exceed those limits. When they reach their limit, they either stop or tip over into metaphysics.

AC: Would you have an example?

BB: Of course. In the current cosmological model, theory manages to trace the entire history of the universe, but stops at a Big Bang: an "appearance" a few fractions of a second after the actual beginning of the universe, which therefore remains totally unexplained.

AC: Physics has not yet said its last word!

BB: In fact, from this point of view, yes! It cannot deal with causes beyond the physical world without stepping outside its native realm—and that is normal. But the cause of the universe is not part of it, it is beyond it, it is metaphysical. Thus, for lack of being able to go back to the cause (unless it leaves physical science behind), a recent theory reports cycles going from *big bang* to *big crunch* (disappearances); and yet, calmly but insistently, the question of their cause

7

continues to be posed. Why then does the universe appear, disappear, and reappear?

AC: What if physics found a material cause for the *big bang*?

BB: Why not? But what will be the cause of this material cause? We then enter into indefinite regressions, sequences of second causes from which we must nevertheless escape. That is, to put it simplistically, alongside the "*how*" there is also the "*why*." In other words, for the natural sciences, the question is to *explain*, whereas for the sciences of the mind, it is to *understand* (Dilthey, 1833–1911). Thus, the sciences are quite effectively concerned with the *how* (allowing us to produce refrigerators and medicines and enabling us to go to the moon), leaving it to metaphysics to be concerned with the *why*. Scientific thought stands complete with technology, whereas metaphysical thought is perpetual.

AC: This, then, is the limit of science: its pragmatic effectiveness. That's not a bad idea.

BB: Absolutely. On the other hand, if it is more a question of knowing than of doing, metaphysics takes back all its rights. Of course, there is scientific knowledge, but this generally has to do with theories provisionally supported by experience, that is to say, more hypotheses or findings than explanations. The *meta*physical ambition lies in the search, the development of an *explanation*.

AC: I understand that science has limits, doesn't metaphysics have any?

The limits of science

BB: Before answering this question, I would like to clarify these limits of science. My understanding is that they are of four orders to be considered.

(1) The first is in the nature of their make-up as science. Each science is defined by an object of study (called its material object) and a perspective (called its formal object). An example will clarify this: agriculture, botany, and pharmacology each have plants as their material object, but one will consider them in terms of farming, another in terms of their structure, and the third in terms of their curative virtues. The same goes for the human body as a material object of medicine, physiology, and anatomy; for the first it is an object of care, for the second the seat of physiological functions, for the third a composition of organs (Chenique, 1927–2012).

AC: And this human body is considered to be composed of matter and form by philosophy…

BB: That's right. And, to conclude this point, since each reality can be considered under several aspects, only its formal object can serve as a principle to specify a science. In doing so, science is constituted, but its limits established.

AC: It's clear. For example: studying an orange with a double decimeter will not give all possible knowledge of the orange.

BB: Exactly.

(2) The second order of the limits of science, I believe, is the reduction relative to quantity only, to the detriment of quality. I mean the mathematization of all sciences in the modern era. Such hybridization with mathematics is particularly visible in basic physics (we have there almost a fusion), but this quantification has become in general a reduction of the

knowledge of things to measurements, whether it is a question of dimensions (your example of the orange and the double decimeter), temperatures, electromagnetism, radioactivity, etc. We have even developed a scientific measurement for love.

AC: It even seems that we have reached the terminus of this measurement approach with quantum physics, where measurements taken influence the outcome of the measurement.

BB: Absolutely. Above all, I think this systematization of measurement and quantification has led to a weakening of the formal object of the sciences—which are increasingly defined simply by their material object, hence their indefinite multiplication: oncology, homological algebra, convex geometry, neurobiology, quantum computing, coleopterology, extragalactic astronomy, arachnology, etc. And there is also this third order of the limits of science:

(3) This third order resides in the limits of knowledge that science has *itself* discovered in the very field of its object. There are:

the *constructive* limits (the famous theorem of Gödel in mathematics or Popper in physics on certainty reduced to a relative confidence towards an hypothesis);

the *predictive* limits (of systems, however deterministic, in mathematics; or the impossibility of predicting with certainty the result of a measurement in quantum physics);

ontological limits (do mathematical objects exist? Is there an independent quantum object with specific properties?);

and *cognitive* limits (in mathematics, whatever the formal system, there is an infinity of true statements that it is impossible to demonstrate; and in physics, quantum mechanics forces us to renounce a description of reality other than that of its phenomenal appearance).

AC: Can't we say it more simply?

BB: Let's say that scientific knowledge is now generally considered scientifically as hypothetical, possible, probable... but is never certain. Of course, the same is not true of the technical applications of the sciences, which are most often reliable and efficient.

(4) But there remains this fourth order of the limits of science. It is a dual one. First of all, among the four causes defined by Aristotle, there is the abandonment of the final cause, the finality, the *why?* already mentioned. What is significant here are the dissenting scientific approaches that attempt to rehabilitate this final cause. We can cite the theory of morphogenetic fields, the anthropic principle or intelligent design. The other aspect is very simple and allows us to enter into metaphysics: that is the difference between existing and being. Science is concerned with what exists, metaphysics, in addition to what exists, is concerned with being.

What is being?

AC: But this distinction made between being and existing seems to involve two synonyms.

BB: But, as you will see, this is so only in appearance. Take a pebble, a rose, a lion, a human being. What is common to them, to the pebble, to the rose, to the lion and to man, is to be. There is being instead of there being nothing.

The stone disappears into dust, the rose dies, the lion and the man too. What remains when they have disappeared is being. They were able to exist, that is to say, they were able to stand up (*sister*) outside (*ex*), because there is being. Being is what allows a "sallying forth from nothingness" (Borella), and without which nothing would exist.

All the things that exist refer to this salience as to their cause. There is a reason for *chose* ("thing" in French) to derive from the Latin *causa* (cause, reason, motive), while *rien* ("nothing" in French) is derived from *rem* (accusative of *res*, "thing" in Latin); things are nothing compared to the being or the cause that underlies them.

We can say that being is a prior necessity, a causality which transcends all existents: a transcendent causality—which is to say a causality that is *beyond* and *above*, that is of a superior order. This is why this being standing behind things is called "God" by many; God is *being*, and still more, as we will see. But there is still something else: what is common to the rose, to the lion, and to man is to live, that is, life, which is why some also call God "the Living One" (Lanza del Vasto, 1901–1981).

AC: I'm beginning to understand what it's all about with metaphysics, but still surprised that God has anything to do with it.

BB: True, modern science excludes God by very nature: "I did not need this hypothesis," the astronomer and physicist Laplace is supposed to have said to Napoleon, refuting Newton's hypothesis of divine interventions in the movements (unexplained at the time) of the planets. But here we must return to the origin of metaphysics. It was a great surprise, in the Christian Middle Ages, to discover that *The Philosopher*, so-called (Aristotle), long before the birth of Christ, had arrived by reason at the existence of God.

Aristotle's metaphysics is a dual science. One side deals with *being as being*, that is to say being beyond any physical being and that in Aristotle has no particular designation. The other side relates to *First Being*, the first unmoved mover or the first cause, arrived at by reasoning. Aristotle calls this side "first philosophy," "wisdom," and "theology" (science of God). These two sides, never confused, constitute a single science in Antiquity and the Middle Ages, until philosophy is separated from theology and the study of being as being comes to be called ontology in the seventeenth century (Clauberg, 1622–1665).

Still today, however, I think metaphysics necessarily encompasses these two sides. God may well be the First Being as he is, above all, the source of being, and as such beyond being and non-being.

AC: Non-being... I am lost.

What about non-being?

BB: Very simply, one cannot reduce God to being. For God, as the cause of being, is necessarily beyond it. Some call God (in this sense) Beyond-Being (Schuon), others Non-Being (Guénon). If the ontological relates to being in general ("being as being" according to Aristotle), in the case of God we enter the superontological (the "beyond of being").

AC: Nothing to do with nothingness!

BB: Absolutely nothing. In our world, because things are not entirely here, because their roots, their source, their cause, are absent here, we also speak of non-being (in lowercase). In a simplified way, the story begins with the Pre-Socratic philosopher Parmenides, for whom, according to his famous statement in his *Treatise on Nature*, "being is, non-being is not." This means that for him there is only being—capable of accessing the truth through the intelligible—and as such immutable, immobile, and exclusive of all non-being. Conversely, Heraclitus asserts that nothing is therefore rather this than that, but everything becomes it. Things are never finished, but are continually being created... Things are assemblages of opposing forces, and the world is a mixture.

And this goes back as well to Plato, who concluded that "non-being is, in a certain respect, and that being in turn, in some way, is not" (*Sophist* 241d), because "being is potency," "capacity for relation."

AC: Isn't that very imprecise?

BB: Admittedly, this is not the ultimate definition of being (which inevitably eludes us), but it reminds us that being is identified both by the idea of identity (its affirmation) and the idea of alterity (its relationship to whatever is not it). A being is both what it is (a lion, for example) and what it is not (a lion is not a dog or a tree, for example), so that there is never a complete definition; and above all, being and non-being are not opposites, but simply other:

> When we state non-being, this is not, it seems, stating something contrary to being, but only something else... Being and the other permeate each other through all genres and interpenetrate each other reciprocally. (*Sophist* 257b, 259a)

AC: With metaphysics, are we therefore still with Plato and Aristotle?

BB: Because they both thought about and established metaphysics, one with, emblematically, his *Parmenides*, the other with his *Metaphysics*, we are condemned to always come back to it. Martin Heidegger, Julius Evola, and Jean Borella, for example, are among the many contemporary metaphysicians who refer to this. Admittedly, more and more sophisticated considerations have been developed over the past 2,500 years, but the fundamentals remain unchanged. The greatest commotions or upheavals took place in the modern era, when, in the eighteenth century, Kant tried to demonstrate that metaphysics was impossible, or when René Guénon (1886–1951), at the beginning of the twentieth century, showed that the possibility of sacred intellectuality was still there.

AC: It will be interesting to talk about this in a future interview. But to conclude this one, in which the limits of science were mentioned, can we ask: are there limits to metaphysics?

The limits of metaphysics

BB: This question leads to an interesting approach. At its simplest: as being concerned with the First Being, the Absolute, or the First Principle, metaphysics must bow before the Unknowable; but this is an absolute limit, and not relative to metaphysics as such. In fact, one can distinguish in metaphysics both what it is as a science and what it is as a path. As a *science*, it can affirm what is in the relationships between the Absolute and the relative. As a *path*, it gives way before its object.

Giving way is even a characteristic peculiar to it. As soon as metaphysics has brought the mind, with the transparency of the intellect, to the reality of things, every concept is abandoned in favor of the thing itself (Aubenque, 1929–2020; Borella). This is knowledge by *participation* as opposed to knowledge by *abstraction*. The gap between subject and object is in a way abolished by this participation, whereas otherwise it is maintained (the subject abstracts a knowledge of the object).

AC: But with participation have we not then passed into the subjective?

BB: On the contrary, this has to do with the intellect's transparency. The intellect is objective by nature—otherwise we would not know what objectivity means (Borella). A man, entirely enclosed in his subjectivity, would not even be able to conceive the notion of subjectivity if he did not have the faculty of objectivity (Schuon, 1907–1998). The animal evolves in an *Umwelt*, an environment; only man, by the nature of his intellect, can posit the world as an objective reality.

AC: Would there not remain at least one apparent limit to mention? This is the fact that "every metaphysical question involves the metaphysician who asks it" (Heidegger, 1889–1976)?

BB: This is what Aristotle already indicated: "it is not intelligence that knows, it is man." If this cannot be interpreted in terms of subjectivity, it is, again, thanks to the transparency of the intellect, its intrinsic objectivity. Intelligence is the sense of reality: the real makes sense to intelligence, just as the visible makes sense to vision and the audible to hearing (Borella). This implication of *who* thinks metaphysics is what makes metaphysics a path, in addition to being a science.

AC: This is what undoubtedly explains the differences between the respective metaphysics of metaphysicians.

BB: Of course. The common point of all metaphysics is this experience of the intellect as a mirror of a light that goes beyond it, that is transcendent to it. The rest is not exempt from personal sensitivities, points of view, interpretations. This ineluctable significance of the individual runs the risk of falling into two distinct pitfalls.

AC: I am most curious! What are these pitfalls?

The pitfalls of metaphysics

BB: I see two major pitfalls in metaphysics. The first consists of a certain intellectual pride: we see only the intelligence embedded in the metaphysical discourse, forgetting that this intelligence is not ours. One thinks oneself above the others, those who do not have access to it intellectually. Happily, the intellect is not the only access to transcendence; hence my article "Do you need to be intelligent to be saved?" (2010).

AC: The answer is in the question!

BB: Yes, of course. And I think that, similarly, to somehow "ape" one or more metaphysicians, be they Plato, Guénon, or Borella, is non-sense.

AC: And the second trap?

BB: This is to build a metaphysical *system*, almost mathematically. That is, to fall back into the merely conceptual, the prison of rational logic, thereby losing sight of the contemplation of essences (Plato), or simply forgetting that the only true light is that which the intellect is simply reflecting.

Chapter 2

Metaphysics and Religion

Given that metaphysics is concerned with God (even under the "secular" labels of First Being or First Principle), one has to ask oneself what distinguishes metaphysics from religion, what distinguishes entry into metaphysics from entry into religion.

AC: In a previous interview, we mentioned elements that lead me to question the possible links between metaphysics and religion. For example, the part of Aristotle's *Metaphysics* concerned with First Being is rightly called "theology" (the study of God), or Plato's placing of the Good "beyond Being." Moreover, we have also spoken of metaphysics as a path, and thus of an "entry" into metaphysics rather as one would speak of an entry into religion. What is your point of view on this?

BB: We could formulate the question as follows: would a metaphysics without God have any meaning? And on this count, I believe there is no way to avoid saying something here about what some have called "the death of God."

Is God really dead?
Some time ago, Nietzsche provoked us with his declaration "God is dead"—to which he added, "and it was we who killed him." So, the way I see it is that he died only for supermen, that is, those—and only those—who see themselves as such.

AC: But isn't the secularization of culture, the disaffection with the churches, well-established?

BB: Certainly, but currently no more so than after the French Revolution (a situation lasting for about fifty years). Nor was this any longer the case at the time of Nietzsche (second half of the nineteenth century), in France in any case. In addition, a recent study shows that a majority of the French remain linked to some religious Confession on the verge of the end of the first quarter of the twenty-first century (more than half are baptized Christians, and ten percent are pious Muslims). Moreover, passing beyond France, and Europe in general, we see that God is not dead for many people. In other words, on the basis of a real and undeniable sociological phenomenon, this current disaffection with the churches in France has more to do with a relative over-interpretation or intellectual construction on the part of philosophers, and apart from that is perhaps a rather short-sighted reading of history.

AC: What philosophers?

BB: Before coming to this, I would like to point out this apparent paradox of the coexistence, at all times and in all places, of believers and unbelievers. For some, the "seers" (Pamphile), God is luminously evident, and yet what they believe in is held by others to be an infantile illusion. Conversely, unbelievers are held to be blind or unconscious, or even, at the very least, inconsistent (Pascal).

AC: Why inconsistent?

BB: This is Pascal's famous "wager": i.e., we have everything to gain by believing; and by unbelief everything to lose (naturally, the reality of this wager itself is still debated). Of course, this reduction to two categories is overly simplistic; there is in fact an almost continuous gradation between the religious fanatic and the ardent atheist (who, between them, represent not even one percent of the world's population). Between these marginal extremes, we find those faithful to a revelation and an instituted Church as well as a whole variety of theist positions (philosophical or religious), deists (of the "natural religion" or "rational religion" type), animists, even instances of a New Age brand of "personal development." As for the so-called side of "unbelief," a similar gradation passes from the rejection of only the institution (while preserving in private a belief in all or part of the revelation), to agnosticism (with different degrees of skepticism), to atheism (indifference), on up to a thoroughgoing antitheism or absolute atheism. Surely, from all this we can conclude that the average believer and unbeliever, who are almost the same person, represent the bulk of the population. Rather than discriminating against people by placing them in categories, this possibility for people to believe or not believe references above all their freedom (and, in Christianity, the grace that bestows faith). Everyone faces the selfsame question, "why is there something rather than nothing?" (Leibniz) or "what was there before?"; and, at the very least, the answer is "I don't know" (cf. *Le Royaume*, Emmanuel Carrère, 1957–).

AC: Alright, here we clearly see the metaphysical approach. But what about the philosophers of the death of God?

BB: "God is dead and it was Kant who killed him!" This was one of my recent conclusions, because I see, in the modern age, the philosophical premises of the death of God in Kant.

AC: But Kant was eminently Christian…

BB: Absolutely, but the death of God will be the consequence of Kant's project of rationalist reduction. According to his philosophy, God becomes inaccessible; therefore, according to him, we need to cure ourselves of mysticism and bring "religion within the limits of simple reason" (the title of his 1793 book). On this basis of the, at best, inaccessibility of a "supernatural," some will pass over to a nonexistent supernatural. Then there is no longer any God, he is dead. And literature follows suit with poets like Heine or Gérard de Nerval in the nineteenth century.

But the extraordinary thing is that the most anti-religious nonetheless end up referring to God or to an Absolute in one way or another. This was the case, immediately after the French Revolution, with the summoning of the "Supreme Being" in the Constitution of 1793 and the worship publicly rendered to him. With a philosopher like Hegel (1770–1831), the death of God is the necessary transition to the deification of man (anthropotheism), the initial negation of God (atheism) being precisely a required transition. With Hegel, Christianity has even become the religion of the exit from religion. And we find this same pattern in sociologists and philosophers like Max Weber or Marcel Gauchet (cf. J.-M. Verlinde, 1947–).

AC: This is the famous "disenchantment of the world" (1904) by Max Weber, since, thanks to science, we can now "master everything by calculation"!

BB: Exactly! Marcel Gauchet will use Weber's formula in two book titles (1985, 1988). Moreover, even very recently (when one would have thought the argument well-rooted), books by philosophers of the death of God keep appearing.

Even dead, God still remains present to them! They can't get rid of him. Then there is *Le religieux après la religion* ("*The Religious after Religion*," Luc Ferry, Marcel Gauchet, 2007), in which the authors see man "completely separated from the divine"—one by exhaustion of the sacred, the other by divinization of man.

In the *Traité d'athéologie* ("Treatise on Atheology," Michel Onfrey, 2005), we find a theory of immanence and a materialist ontology. This is a very militant book, like those that appear in English, of the ilk of *The God Delusion* (2006) by Richard Dawkins; however, the latter is not a philosopher, but an evolutionary biologist.

AC: A biologist who speaks about God, is he not mistaken about science, given what we have seen on this theme?

BB: Yes, absolutely. For him, man is "a survival-machine, a robot programmed blindly to preserve selfish molecules called genes"; this point of view is interesting biologically, but does not hold philosophically. While Darwin explicitly left room for God, his disciple Dawkins is very upset about religion and goes so far as to write that a Catholic education is worse than pedophilia! Here we have a case where scientific interpretation is distorted by ideology. There was also the case of the great theoretical physicist and cosmologist Stephen Hawking with a book co-written with physicist Leonard Mlodinow (*The Grand Design*, 2010/2011) that in terms of philosophy and of science in the strict sense, seems rather inept.

AC: Actually, all we have to do is read the *Answer to Stephen Hawking: From Physics to Science Fiction* by physicist Wolfgang Smith that we published in 2013...

BB: Back to the philosophers. Onfray's book was very controversial, especially for its historical errors and a misunderstanding of religions—which were reduced to a "deathwish"! Here too, ideology takes the place of philosophy. On the other hand, he is right to denounce the secular neo-religious perversion, but he interprets it as an obstacle to a true atheism that he wishes for with all his might, whereas I interpret it rather as the metaphysical impossibility of ridding man of God.

AC: Do you have in mind an example of this secular neo-religious perversion?

BB: We have mentioned the cult of the Supreme Being after the French Revolution. Today, typically, we see "secular baptisms" in town halls, secular wedding celebrations parodying religious marriages, and we have this famous fashionable "living together," which is a poor substitute for charity, while the absence of any basis for all this renders these "rites" pretty much ineffectual. Even a Voltaire had already conceded:

> What would become of the world & society,
> If everything, even the Atheist, was without charity?

and confessed shortly before his death: "I believe in *a* God, however, since I have to tell you so." In *L'Esprit de l'athéisme* ("The Spirit of Atheism," Comte-Sponville, 2006), we find this same transposition of the religious into the secular. For example, the "sanctity of atheists" (which consists in being satisfied with the merely human); the preservation and transmission of "Judeo-Christian values," but in a secular form, because "nothing has meaning except that which is invented out of love"! On the strength of a "mystical" experience in his youth (the famous "oceanic feeling" of Romain

Rolland taken up by Freud), this philosopher sees in it an "indissoluble union with the great All" ("all" with a capital A!). "We are already in the Kingdom," he writes. His "spirituality without God" is therefore not without the divine, even if reduced to its immanence.

Moreover, appealing to an eastern spirituality, he puts this immanence in the "humanity" common to human beings, so that no one seems personally involved in an undifferentiated Whole. This is a spirituality without God... and without a subject (J.-M. Verlinde).

AC: Can you remind us about the meaning of immanence?

BB: It is simple and important to understand it. What is immanent in a thing or in a being does not come from an external principle, but originates in it. The opposite is "transcendent," that is to say whatever belongs to a superior order of reality, to an external and superior principle. If we are speaking about God, He is necessarily both immanent (present in everything) and transcendent (beyond everything). This is one of the essential paradoxes in metaphysics and, of course, in theology. To illustrate, according to *L'Esprit de l'athéisme*, there is no principle behind the values immanent to humanity; they "appear"! This observation suffices to satisfy this philosopher.

Let us quote a final book, *L'homme-Dieu* ("Man-God," Luc Ferry, 1996), in which we no longer have something divine immanent within humanity, but this time a "transcendental humanism"—that is, under another name, Nietzsche's Superman. "The human is excess or it is not," says the author (repeating Pascal: "man goes infinitely beyond man"). However, for lack of a basis for the values he recognizes as the Good, the Beautiful, and especially Love,

25

these remain a "mystery at the heart of the human being"; they create the sacred or the divine in man; this is an "immanent transcendence"!

AC: Isn't that an oxymoron?

BB: Yes, it's hard to understand. Especially since, ultimately, it is the Charter of Human Rights (but without the Supreme Being!) which, for this philosopher, will best summarize these universal human values!

My conclusion is that these different philosophers, who are not metaphysicians, are mostly anticlerical, and on the basis of an affirmation like the death of God interpret episodic and regional sociological phenomena according to their own belief and according to an unfinished philosophical construction. This is of course just an opinion.

AC: Finally, should we believe that God is dead or believe in him?

BB: I believe that what history teaches, above all, is the freedom of man *vis-à-vis* God. As for the "existence of God," I think that this point deserves a specific interview.

AC: Noted!

BB: Let's proceed, then, with this theme of metaphysics and religion, contenting ourselves with agreeing that nothing is without cause, that the cause is transcendent to the effects, and that man is capable of thinking about God independently of religion, as Aristotle's "theology" bears witness.

The languages of metaphysics and religion

I would say that it is first of all a question of language. Religions, revelations, appear in particular cultural basins, in places, that is, where (philosophical) thought and the sacred already exist. That goes without saying. But the consequence is the necessary relative adaptation of one to the other, and this takes place through concepts, and therefore language. Christianity thus "absorbed" a certain Platonism (St Augustine retaining the intelligible forms of Plato and, naturally, placing them in the Word, the divine Logos), as well as a certain Aristotelianism (St Thomas Aquinas, in the Middle Ages, "integrating" Aristotle into Christian metaphysics).

AC: How can two such divergent visions of the world be made compatible? One, that of Plato, seeing in the world an icon, a symbol, or, simply, an image of the divine; the other, that of Aristotle, for whom the world is entirely *there*;—you just have to measure it to know it.

BB: Yes, this gap, even this wide gap, is very real. But there is also a complementarity. One brings the metaphysical and almost mystical vision of what is "far beyond being," the other offers metaphysical concepts still used today.

AC: Potency and act...

BB: Precisely. And God alone is pure act in Aristotle, as in Christianity. This is an example of a concept of metaphysical language that is readily common to philosophy and religion (Christianity here, in any case).

The distinction between metaphysics and esotericism will be enlightening in terms of language. Esotericism, with its play of symbols and analogies, shows that there is a veil, and that this veil masks a hidden Reality; by contrast, metaphysics operates directly behind the veil (Borella). It uses the language of intelligence: concepts, principles, logic; and, thanks to the transparency of intelligence, points to what is beyond language and concepts, to ultimate reality.

From this point of view, metaphysics is the ultimate herme-
neutic (or interpretation), which can no longer be interpreted in turn (Borella).

AC: But metaphysics also speaks in symbols...

BB: Yes, in addition to the intellectual mode, metaphysics
also calls on the symbolic mode. They are complementary:
the symbolic makes us see, the intellect makes us hear
(Borella). Now for a fundamental point: if our intelligence
can speak just as well about natural things as about supernatural things, this is because it is naturally nowhere. This
is why Aristotle says that "the intellect comes through the
door" or "from outside." Hence the end of metaphysics,
which for the metaphysician is the renunciation of his own
intelligence, of his little light. Hence also the ultimate
renunciation of all discourse, which is pointed to by the
transparency of metaphysical language. By disappearing, it
gives the intellect access to the reality beyond it, access to
the light of truth that never resides in words (Aubenque,
Borella).

AC: So what is the difference between metaphysics and
religion?

BB: As a science, metaphysics is primarily a philosophical
discipline, but as a language, anyone can speak it, the philosopher as well as the theologian. Above all, metaphysics is
not just a science, it is also a way, a path. This is where the
simple level of discursive reason *à la* Aristotle can be com-
pleted by that of illuminative intelligence *à la* Plato. This is
the superiority of Plato over Aristotle. There, metaphysics
becomes somehow mystical.

From this point of view, metaphysics is at home in all

religions; their language is also made up of concepts and symbols. This is universal and illustrated by a hadith...

AC: Hadith?

BB: Hadiths, in Islam, are the deeds or words of the Prophet Muhammad. This particular hadith reports the saying: "I stand, says God, in the ideas that my servant has of me." I understand it as the chance given to everyone to approach God, beyond all the imperfections of language, concepts, clumsy—or simply approximate—ideas that one may have of Him.

AC: So there is, from this point of view, an equivalence of all religions?

BB: In a way and up to a point, yes. But, if certain intellectual tools and symbols can be common to several religions, this is not the case for all, far from it. That is to say, very specifically, that there is no universal metaphysics, common to all religions, even if we no longer count the analogies revealed by the comparative study of religions. Above all, there is no supra-metaphysics, above religions.

AC: Yet it was very tempting, and why?

BB: We will see this later. But, for now, take the two famous attempts of the twentieth century. There was that of the metaphysician Frithjof Schuon (1907–1998) who affirmed *The Transcendent Unity of Religions* (this is the title of his 1953 book, revised in 1975) in reference to a *Religio perennis* (perennial religion), a "metaphysical religion" he sees as "the quintessence of all religion." The problem is that a religion without revelation cannot be one; it may have the flavor, but not the substance of one (Borella). And of course, Schuon never claimed to be himself either the revealer or the prophet of this religion. Another difficulty lies in the transcendence of this unity: it is placed above all religions. However, I believe that above religions there is only God, no place for anything else. This is what Ramakrishna (1836–1886) said: "Religions flow into God like rivers into the sea." And this access to God is known: it is called *gnosis*. However, it does not come from the "metaphysical" efforts of man, but solely from the good will of God. Schuon recognizes a metaphysical revelation that actualizes the intellective faculty, of course; but this is not a revelation of God as such, it is only the *awareness* of any metaphysician discovering the transparency of the intellect. This one is a crystal, but it is only a crystal, it will never create by itself the light capable of illuminating it.

AC: Wouldn't it be better, then, to speak of the immanent unity of religions, or better yet, of the analogical unity of religions (Borella)?

BB: Absolutely. Moreover, one of the titles initially planned was "On the convergence of traditional forms," which is less debatable, even though there is no analogy to the Christian Trinity in Islam or Judaism (Schuon, Schaya). My conclusion is that the mystery of the existence of multiple religions is best left to God. Origen spoke of the "condescensions" (*sugkatabasis*) of God towards the different parts of humanity. Cultures are oriented by the revelations that occur there, and these cultures then shape the religions that develop there. Who could with certainty unravel all this?

AC: Not me (laughs)! On this example, we understand in any case that metaphysics cannot be above religions. And what is the second example?

BB: Here we have the metaphysician René Guénon (1886–

1951). He speaks of a "primordial tradition" (*Sanatana Dharma* in Hinduism) that he illustrates by the existence of prehistoric symbols, prior to known religions, as well as by symbols common to several traditions (roughly, he renames religions "traditions").

AC: His works on symbols and esotericism are unequaled, but could we be faced with this classic error of the historian seeking a common origin for identical phenomena?

BB: No, his approach is not historicist, and he sees that the origin of symbolism merges with the origin of humanity, and even of the world—the order of nature symbolizing the order of principles.

Every human being, at all times and in all places, has understood that he was not his own cause, and that everything claimed a cause until it reached a cause without a cause (simple discursive reason achieves this—*cf.* Aristotle), and many human beings, if not all of them (even if confusedly) were able to think mystically of that which is "far beyond being" (Plato in this instance). *Homo religiosus* is for me something anthropologically evident that can do without hypothetical studies either of Paleolithic man or further back, say, three million years ago. Personally, I would put the initialization of such a "primordial tradition" at the creation of Adam and Eve, at the creation of the human being.

It should be added that Guénon affirmed the existence of a "King of the World," guarantor of this primordial tradition through the ages. His metaphysics is remarkable, but this account remains debatable (Jean-Pierre Laurant, 1935).

AC: With this story by itself, one has the impression of being more in the realm of esotericism than of metaphysics.

BB: Yes exactly. The notion of the center of the world is

widespread, especially in Asia: Shambhala for example (James George, 1919–2020), but this center is wherever the vertical axis crosses the horizontal plane of manifestation; it is "within you" (Luke 17:21), says Christianity (and Hinduism as well).

In summary, I would say that where Schuon seems to construct a metaphysical religion above religions, Guénon sees one, prior to known religions, which become in turn resurgences of it. Moreover, whether true or false, the secret existence of a "King of the World" is of no consequence to us. Again, if it is simply a question of thinking that man has always been "religious," the answer is only too obvious. Can we see further? For a Buddhist, a Christian, a Muslim today, this protohistoric anteriority, including its possible present interest, is, I believe, useless.

AC: How would you like to end this interview?

Christian metaphysics

BB: I would like to conclude on what a Christian metaphysics is, which in my view will answer this question of the relationship between metaphysics and religion. First and foremost, such a metaphysics necessarily develops *within* Christianity. Therefore, it is not a philosophical interpretation of Christianity, but a metaphysical formulation of the Christian mysteries themselves. Thus, as an integral metaphysics, it does not stop at a discursive reason *à la* Aristotle, but includes a "mystical" intellectuality *à la* Plato. Hence, it is necessarily the work of a Christian. Which explains why it is to be found in our readings of St Augustine, St Dionysius the Areopagite, St Thomas Aquinas, Meister Eckhart, Silesius, Duns Scotus, and hundreds of others. It also explains how such an integral metaphysics is somewhat distorted in Guénon, whose knowledge of Christianity seems to have been in some ways lacking, despite the intellectual power of his metaphysics.

AC: Hence, perhaps, his conversion to Islam?

BB: Quite possibly. Guénon was a great metaphysician, but ultimately not a Christian. We have the opposite example with Kant, a good Christian, but an anti-metaphysician when he wished to confine "religion within the limits of simple reason" at the time when the French Revolution had launched a cult to the goddess Reason—a sign of the times! But if religion is deprived of its access to the supernatural, is it still a religion?

AC: And vis-à-vis theology?

BB: It suffices to read a few texts by St Dionysius the Areopagite, a few sermons by Meister Eckhart, or a few passages from the *Summa Theologica* of St Thomas Aquinas. There is nothing to envy in Vedanta or Buddhism, however sublime the metaphysics found there may be. The metaphysical approach is particularly at home in theology, especially since its "mystical" aim meets revelation there. In a way, Plato has encountered Christ there.

AC: We can therefore say that the metaphysical approach, as a non-confessional means, is in its place when put at the service of theology.

BB: I believe one can even say that despite the academic schools of philosophy, where metaphysics of course has its place, theology is its place of predilection. What would a metaphysics reputed to be complete, that is to say "mystical" *à la* Plato, be without dealing with the Beyond? And what would it be if it were deprived of the possibility of

33

being silent, of giving way to the things towards which it tends by its simple constitution as science, as nescience even (Aubenque, Borella)?

AC: Why "nescience"?

BB: "Nescience" precisely allows us to remember that the paradox of metaphysics is that it functions like a science with its own language capable of formulating the ultimate; but, once this ultimate has been formulated, it gives access to it. It's the end of the road, after which the road no longer has any interest.

And here is something even better. We have seen that metaphysical thoughts can contribute to religion: this is the case when Christianity integrates Plato or Aristotle. But if religion does integrate metaphysics, this is because there is a conjunction between the language of metaphysics and the mysteries of revelation. But above all, the reverse is also true: there is a metaphysics we reach thanks to Christian language that we would never have reached without it.

AC: An example?

BB: The Trinity! It identifies person and relationship. The persons of the Father and the Son turn out to be pure relations (paternity and filiation)—otherwise there would not be one God. Conversely, the relationship of Love and Gift between the Father and the Son turns out to be a Person: the Holy Spirit. The human being is also first of all relations: that which connects him to the One who gives him being, to his parents (otherwise he would be a feral child) and to all the others, whether he meets them or not, that make up the human world. We can then move from a classic metaphysics of being to a metaphysics of relation. Being is first of all relational.

Chapter 3
Metaphysics and Mysticism

Intrigued by this comparison, since it allows us to better distinguish a discipline from a spiritual path, I selected this theme among those mentioned in one of our interviews.

AC: During one of our interviews, you mentioned an editorial project that would be entitled "Metaphysics and Mysticism" and about which you said nothing. The title of course is by design somewhat provocative, at least intriguing. Can you talk about it?

BB: Of course. It's a very simple project, which would fit in one paragraph, if it were not as well an opportunity to study the metaphysics of mystics as well as the mysticism of metaphysicians.

Rational metaphysics and mystical metaphysics
We have seen that the metaphysical theology of Aristotle was a rational theology, while the mystical metaphysics of Plato went beyond this reduction. Everything is there; it is of course simplified, but in no way simplistic. The mind of man is endowed with two faculties: a reason, that is to say an organ of calculation…

AC: What do you mean?

BB: Not so long ago, a *liber rationis* or *liber rationum* ("book of reason") was an accounting book. And, as logic tells us, propositions are to be *calculated*. Reason, of course, is far from negligible; it allows the "reasonable animal" to acquire hypothetico-deductive knowledge through discursive reason. This is termed *dianoia*, and the prefix *dia* marks the distance maintained between subject and object. Such knowledge by abstraction (whether conceptual or mathematical) has an illusory, even "*dia*bolical" side—of course, not in practical or technical terms, but at the bottom line is that really a knowledge? No, it is most often observation, at best a descriptive one (such as the force of gravity), but never an intimate understanding of reality.

The second instance, which we have also already mentioned, is intelligence, the immediate cognitive process of intuitive apprehension or, as Plato proposes, the dialectical ascent of the intellect reaching this intuitive knowledge. This is termed *noesis*.

AC: This is the line of analogy shown in Appendix I.

BB: Yes, we always come back to it. This access to the real, which is the sense of the intellect, makes it possible to think about God, not rationally as with Aristotle, but intuitively, comprehensively. It is the *noesis* distinguished by Plato from discursive reason, *dianoia*.

AC: Every human being has these two faculties, even this "dual faculty," as you said; but when we see how human beings give priority to one or the other of these two faculties, can we discern a predisposition of the mind? This is even what we saw with St Thomas Aquinas compared to St Bonaventure, whose views "neither exclude or coincide" (Étienne Gilson, 1884–1978).

BB: Yes, the first demonstrates [*démontre*] because it abstracts, the second shows [*montre*] because it recognizes (Henry Duméry, 1920–2012). A philosopher has said this in yet another way by distinguishing "philosophies of truth and philosophies of reality." The former seek the causes to demonstrate the truth, the latter seek the source to show the reality: "the source is on the level of reality what the cause is on the level of truth." (Henri Gouhier, 1898–1994)

AC: Can you explain?

BB: The philosophies of truth start from the real, reason about the existing data, what is given, and focus on explaining it by looking for the non-given principles that lie beyond it. Explaining and demonstrating what is explicable and demonstrable, they discard the irrational and somehow rationalize what is able to be rationalized within reality. For the philosophies of reality, on the other hand, as the real is not *accessible* to reason, their goal is to *approach* it. A successful exploration following this approach can never be proven, but once discovered, it will be a matter of showing it. What is not rational cannot be explained, but remains showable.

AC: These two approaches are of course complementary, and any philosophy that does not participate in both cannot be, well, a philosophy, either because it would be an irrational communion with reality, or because its rational systems of truths would remain wordy, disconnected from all reality. But I come back to my question, is there not some mental or spiritual predisposition in this?

BB: Yes, we can distinguish two very different forms of spirit: the mind-set of *implication* and the mind-set of *consecution*. For the first, things are included in each other and linked together: St Bonaventure is of this type, inclined to synthesis. The second form is more prone to analysis: St Thomas Aquinas, for example (Chenique).

That said, as you indicated, the dual approach is necessary for any integral thought; this is why St Thomas Aquinas quotes St Dionysius the Areopagite much more than he does Aristotle. The way things are presented allows us to distinguish a mind-set of implication from one of consecution.

AC: So how can we conclude on this first theme?

BB: I would say that this already mentioned "kernel of gnosis" is common to all people; otherwise nothing would make sense to anyone. When, in Plato's *Sophist* for example, the sophist asserts that his speech creates the true or the false, he forgets that for his assertion to be intelligible, "true" and "false" must mean exactly what they mean (Plato, Borella).

Very prosaically, if metaphysics is concerned with the beyond of physics, with the beyond of nature (the supernatural), it is necessarily "mystical": the intelligence reflects a light that it cannot create by itself—that is the intelligibility of things we perceive thanks to an "intellect [that] comes from outside" (Aristotle). In this, all metaphysics is necessarily "mystical," since, even as metaphysics, its discourse refers to a beyond of the physical world, in which it believes; otherwise it would fall silent.

AC: We can still read of this gap between *dianoia* and *noesis* today, in Krishnamurti (1895–1986) for example, when he says: "Penetrating vision is not the meticulous deduction of thought. It is perception without the perceiver." My question is: how then can we talk about it? What to say?

What can be said of the inexpressible?

BB: It has been rightly said that mystery is not the incomprehensible, but the inexpressible (Chenique), and the etymology of "mystery" confirms this: the word comes from "mute." A few philosophers in the modern era have also said that nothing could be said about it: Kant (1724–1804), by decreeing any knowledge beyond the limits of simple reason impossible; Wittgenstein (1889–1951), with his instruction: "That of which we cannot speak, we must pass over in silence" (*Tractatus logico-philosophicus*, 1919), that is to say everything that is of the aesthetic, religious, ethical, or metaphysical order; or even Heidegger (1889–1976) who, by saying there was no real metaphysics before him—since it would only have dealt with beings and never yet with being itself—belittles Aristotle and quite simply ignores Plato.

AC: Fortunately, there was Guénon, Schuon, Étienne Gilson, Borella... to at least remind us of the possibility of this already mentioned knowledge by participation. But the question remains: "what can we say about the unspeakable?"

BB: There is already, common to almost all human beings, the recognition of a transcendent principle (i.e., beyond and superior) to the universe we know. This is the answer contained in Leibniz's question: "why is there something rather than nothing?" Everything has a cause, any science is knowledge through causes, and there is necessarily a Cause without a cause, a First Cause—the unmoved mover of Aristotle, to which the simple study of nature leads.

AC: And what about chance?

BB: From this point of view, the cause is in the establishment of the environment in which chance can occur, such as the programmer of the algorithm proposing random occurrences.

AC: Doesn't the idea of an eternal return make it possible to dispense with a first cause, the end of one cycle causing the beginning of the next?

BB: First, an eternal return to the strictly same would mean one single cycle only, and if they are different there is therefore no eternal return *per se* (Borella). Also, the cause of the existence of this cycle or these cycles remains necessary.

AC: And can we say something more about this transcendent cause?

BB: Two more or less convergent approaches are available to us. A more "deductive" or "constructive" approach, and a more "receptive" one. The first lists all the necessary attributes of the Principle from what is manifested, because the Principle, as a source, must necessarily contain all the foundations like love, intelligence, power, etc. The second is what a revelation and the tradition associated with it says.

AC: It gives the impression that metaphysics and religions are on an equal footing, right?

BB: Actually, the constructive/deductive approach requires a minimum of "receptivity" or intellectual intuition, otherwise the concepts developed would not make sense. There is a rational "dressing"—but one must not be fooled by this: the fact that the "notion" of God makes sense, governs the whole project. The fundamental difference between these two approaches lies in the awareness we have, or do not have, of the light we receive. This consciousness can be called faith if it becomes confidence in the revelation and tradition of a religion; yet even if we do not have this consciousness, there nevertheless remains this famous "kernel of gnosis" (Borella), common to all human beings.

AC: In fact, we can no more do without intelligence than we could do without reason. The key point is: which of these two "authorities" will take precedence?

BB: We can frame this in a somewhat similar way. There is a risk in giving precedence to reason: it gives too much importance to one's own little individual light, which is only a reflection of that "true Light, which lighteth every man that cometh into the world" (John 1:9), to put it in Christian language.

AC: Could you cite some examples?

BB: Simply put, without the light that illuminates it, Kant has granted to reason far more than it can offer; but that did not prevent him from being a "good Christian." Likewise, all the modern metaphysicians we have cited, Guénon, Schuon, Schaya, Burckhardt, Coomaraswamy, Chenique, Borella, have been religious (Islam, Hinduism, Christianity).

AC: To be a metaphysician is therefore to be religious!

BB: This is what the understanding of the lights of intelligence seems to indicate, as well as the example of the metaphysicians mentioned. Personally, that's what I think. The approach of Heidegger (1889–1976), it seems to me, reinforces to absurdity this position: he departs from his Catholic faith in favor of a "methodological atheism." For him, "philosophy is itself and as such atheist"; and this is what allows it to be a science. We find here both the Aristotelian scientific reduction and the precedence given to reason as in Kant. But is not the "atheizing" of philosophy quite simply a severing of philosophy from its transcendent source and thereby, paradoxically, recognizing this source?

41

AC: Heidegger was nevertheless a metaphysician!

BB: Yes, but metaphysics begins with him, he claims. Hence his critique that everything preceding him was only concerned with beings (the existents) and not with being as such: this "sallying forth outside of nothing" (Borella). By dealing with being qua being, he is a metaphysician, whereas in all the metaphysics of the past he has seen only the naturalism of Aristotelianism. He missed Platonism! My conviction is that he used the "spectacles" of his own approach to reduce philosophy to a science. Following him, Quine (1908–2000) will see no difference between science and philosophy; for him, propositions and ideas are calculated in the latter.

AC: We calculate, but then we no longer think! If I understand this correctly, considered schematically, we are either Aristotelian and rationalize external data, or as Platonists the awareness or intuition of the transcendent is obvious. This is why the aforesaid proofs of the existence of God are useless, right?

Proofs of the existence of God

BB: Talking about proof means taking a more rational or logical approach, and without doubt these proofs have been useful—at least to those who have developed them.

AC: In other words?

BB: In other words, although having the *intuition* of a Cause of causes, they nevertheless pursue a work of *rationality.* This leads them to logical reasoning, allowing them to reconcile their dual faculty: intellectual intuition and discursive reason. My thesis is that, first and foremost, this is a work of internal conciliation. The danger then is to give the apparent primacy to reason.

AC: I see. And what are these "proofs"?

BB: Broadly speaking, these proofs are what are called "logically grounded thought experiments" and are related to the experience one may have of the outside world.

There are three classic proofs (Aristotle, St Thomas Aquinas, William L. Craig, 1949–) that start from the experience of the contingency of the world and infer therefrom the necessary existence of God (hence their name "cosmological proofs"). There is the famous unmoved mover (all movement being caused by a mover, there must necessarily be a first motionless mover, that is, not moved by another). We also prove the existence of such a mover. Finally, there is the approach by contingency and necessity (since everything is not strictly contingent, there is at least one being whose existence is necessary and thus not made necessary by another).

AC: And that's all?

BB: Almost, there are two other classic proofs. One, distinguishing some finality in the universe, concludes with the necessity of an intelligent being by which all natural things are ordered to their end. We find it first in Plato, but also in Aristotle, al-Kindi (801–873), St Thomas Aquinas, Leibniz, and even Voltaire (1694–1778)!

AC: These are his famous verses:

> The universe embarrasses me, and I cannot think
> That this clock exists and has no watchmaker. (*Les cabales*, 1772)

BB: This argument was even mentioned in 1734. In the

Anglo-Saxon world, this argument is known as the "Great watchmaker" (the watchmaker analogy), the inventor of which is surprisingly held to be William Paley (1743–1805), in 1802!

AC: This teleological argument is never found in science?

BB: It is no longer found except in heterodox finalist scientific options, such as intelligent design or the arguments of irreducible complexity (Behe, 1952–) and of specified complex information (Dembski, 1960–), or the anthropic principle (Carter, 1942–), or, again, the theories of morphogenetic fields (Sheldrake, 1942–) and demonstrated vertical causality (Wolfgang Smith, 1930–2024).

And they are not philosophers. Whatever their skills in metaphysics, they are essentially scientists.

AC: And what about such cases?

BB: On the terrain of finality, philosophy has rights that science does not have, or no longer has. Modern science has in fact, by method, excluded from its field of research the final cause established by Aristotle. It would take something enormous to change that…

There still is this other proof by perfections. Having identified different degrees of perfection in nature, we infer the necessary existence of an absolute perfection. We find this reasoning, at least sketched, in Plato and Aristotle, then in St Augustine, St Thomas Aquinas, Bossuet (1627–1704)…

AC: It seems that with all these "proofs," we have two basic metaphysical notions: the need for causality or sufficient reason (Leibniz; Clarke, 1675–1729) and the fact that everything requires a principle that is superior to it, and even a first Principle possessing all perfections. Sounds pretty undeniable, right?

44

BB: Everything can always be denied—and has been—but there is still one argument to add to the list. This is the so-called moral proof of Kant: God is the only possible reason for moral conscience (*Critique of Practical Reason*, 1788), a proof we find as well in St John Henry Newman (1801–1890), Maurice Nédoncelle (1905–1976), or in Craig's work. Still, Kant denied all the other proofs and replaced them with this one.

AC: What arguments did he use?

BB: In Kant, we are always situated in the denial of an intellectual intuition that overhangs reason and makes its calculations intelligible. Reason is left with the objects to which it has access. It therefore depends strictly on it, as well as on the strict logic to which it is submitted (Borella). Now, in all the arguments that start from the world and deduce God from it, there is, for him, this necessary but impossible thought of the existence of God; therefore, for Kant, all these proofs are invalid. As we can see, he is a prisoner of his rationalist scheme: the concept of God is identical whether he exists or not. He thus reduces the cognizable to the conceivable…

AC: Could you explain further?

BB: For him, all true knowledge must be conceptual and all concepts require an empirical guarantee. Thus, one can only think by concept. Therefore, to think God is to think a concept, on which, strictly speaking, one cannot superimpose an existence.

AC: But does he not then commit this error when he thinks the existence of God necessary to the moral conscience?

BB: His thesis on pure reason no longer applies to practical reason. For morals and good manners, it is very practical that God exists. However, we cannot know anything about it, we can only believe in it. Very generally, I believe he fell into the trap of his immense intelligence, ceding all his confidence to his own light alone. Once the construction of his work had begun, he found himself condemned to follow his logic to the end. Conversely, St Thomas Aquinas, whose intellectual power is obvious, was able to affirm, as we have already mentioned, that his colossal and unequaled work was only straw (compared to an experience of God).

AC: Are there any others beside Kant to refute all these proofs of the existence of God?

BB: They are surely innumerable in a world where there have always been those who tend to believe and those who tend not to believe. Moreover, this existence of unbelievers has even been an argument against the existence of God. In the modern world there are many arguments, often coming from scientists: verificationism which would like God to be tested empirically (Carnap, 1891–1970), rational logic defining that the burden of proof is on the one who affirms God's existence (Russell, 1872–1970). There is also the argument of a superfluous God to explain the world (Laplace, 1749–1827; Hawking, 1942–2018), which however would not prevent Him from existing (van Inwagen, 1942–).

AC: This is all tied to the belief in a science capable of explaining everything…

BB: Yes, we have already talked about it. But such a principled stand also consists in noting that something exists, and being satisfied with this observation. Hawking can say: "if the Universe is completely autonomous, without borders or edges, it can neither be created nor destroyed. It is, that's all." (*Little History of the Universe*, 2008) Such a universe has no raison d'être, but that is fair enough for him.

There are still a few arguments to be raised: the one of the imperfect world (against Leibniz's "best of all possible worlds"), the one of the presence of evil, or even the denunciation of a God-illusion ("man created God in his image," said Feuerbach)...

AC: That's the crux of the matter, isn't it? The fact that any criticism by way of universal illusion either puts the one who discovers it above all humanity, or else the illusion is not universal!

BB: Yes, it is a trap into which many have fallen; to the societal illusion denounced by Feuerbach (1804–1872) corresponded the psychological illusion affirmed by Freud (1856–1939). More recently, we find neurological arguments: thinking of God activates the medial prefrontal cortex (Nicholas Epley); religiosity is due to the neurotransmitter called serotonin (Jacqueline Borg); the sensation of fusion with the universe comes from a slowing down of activity of the superior parietal cortex; the divine presence makes its appearance under electromagnetic stimulation of the temporal lobes (Michael Persinger); the impression of leaving the body is obtained by activating the angular gyrus of the temporal cortex (Olaf Blanke)...

AC: And what should we think of all this?

BB: The continuity between psychic and physical states and their reciprocal influences no longer needs to be demonstrated. I think that this physical anchorage of human life does not determine either freedom or conscience, which go hand in hand.

Above all, there is something more interesting than all these rational proofs of God, starting from the experience of the world and going back to its cause, as with Aristotle. There is the experience of the Idea of God—with a capital "I"—as with Plato.

AC: This capital "I" is essential. There we are no longer in the domain of simple ideas—lowercase "i"—or concepts: i.e., the realm of rationality, but in intelligible reality.

BB: And we "access" it when the intellect reflects this reality, and when we realize that it is a reflection and not our own light.

Experiences of God

Such experiences of God have been related by metaphysicians since at least Plato. For our own era, we should mention the initiator St Anselm (1033/1034–1109), known as the "magnificent doctor," then Descartes, Leibniz, and Borella, for what I know of them.

Descartes' version is famous, because it is the one that will be misunderstood by Kant and, as a matter of fact, by Schopenhauer. For Descartes, to think of God is not to think of a being so perfect that one would otherwise miss his existence; rather, God *is* because we can think him. As a metaphysician, he remains in the same vein as that of the *Cogito* (which says in fact: it is because I think that I am). Thus, far from an "I think God, therefore he exists," he realizes that "it is because God is, that I can think him":

> This idea is innate in me. God in creating me, placed this idea in me to be like the mark of the workman imprinted on his work. (*Meditations on First Philosophy*, 1641)

Kant called this the "ontological proof," because he saw it as a concept to which existence has been added. Yet Descartes makes it clear that his thought does not create existence, but that it is "the existence of God [which] determines me to have this thought"; God is not a concept, except in Kantianism, or, as Kant himself puts it: "no man could, by mere ideas, become richer in knowledge."

AC: It is always this Platonic distinction between concept or idea (lowercase "i") and intelligible reality or the world of Ideas (capital "I").

BB: A distinction that Aristotle rightly did not want to consider in order to found science and that Kant wishes to apply to philosophy. Above all, for Kant, it is a matter of separating the order of being from that of thought. But if we admit then that these two orders are completely foreign to each other, two cases will arise:

> if this radical separation pertains to the order of being (and therefore is true), Kant's thought can miraculously come out of itself: here we have that intuition whose possibility he denies;

> if this separation still pertains to the order of thought, the being in question is a thought being, and consequently it is even absolutely impossible to know whether one can pass from the logical to the ontological or not, since the ontological is never anything but ontological thinking, that is to say logical thinking (Borella).

AC: This is clearly the contradiction of the Kantian system. He can only speak about the being that is thought, unless he has a certain intuition about it. But that possibility he

49

denies.

BB: To mask this contradiction, he distinguishes thinking and knowing; but this is only true of the absolute; for everything else, as we have said, intelligence is the sense of reality and thus the orders of being and thought are not strangers to each other: "there is being only for knowledge" (Borella).

It is absolutely necessary to say a word about the experiment proposed by St Anselm (of Canterbury). He too never claimed to link concept and existence: "It is indeed another thing to have the idea of any object, another thing is to believe in its existence."

Rather, he proposes to share his experience of thinking about God, such that he cannot conceive of anything greater. The question is to find what will put an end to the conceptual increase of the greatest possible. The being of God, the fact that he is, is not one of the various perfections that can be added to him, but the integrality of all possible perfections, precisely because he is considered pure and infinite Reality, the unsurpassable limit of thought.

AC: But aren't we still in the realm of thought?

BB: Yes, in a certain way, and this is what St Thomas Aquinas said: "From what one conceives of what the word God expresses, it does not follow that God exists, if this is not in the intellect." (*Contra Gentiles*, L. I, chap. 11) However, it is not by nature, as in Kant, but because we do not really comprehend the divine essence owing to the weakness of our intellect: the existence of God is *obvious by itself*, but not obvious for us, says St Thomas Aquinas.

AC: And how could the existence of God be both self-evident and not self-evident to us? It's ever and always just we ourselves who are thinking, whether we're called Anselm, Thomas, Leibniz, Descartes, or Kant! (Borella)

BB: That's the right question. Is it not impossible to think of God as necessary, while thinking that this necessity is purely ideal and not real? Either this thought attains to being and the truth in one way or another—and our discourses have a meaning—or else they do not, in which case the refutation of the discourses of St Anselm or Descartes is only another meaningless discourse (Borella).

Of course, the experiment proposed by St Anselm is not a rational demonstration. It is not a question of demonstrating [*démontrer*], but of showing [*montrer*]. St Anselm does not offer a proof, but a test (Borella). By carrying out the act of the highest possible conception, one subjects the intelligence to such a speculative effort that it is obliged to surpass itself, to abandon its paltry conceptual light for a beyond. The experimenter then ceases to think for himself and allows himself to be thought by What is thought in him. He is no longer the cause of thought, but his thought is an effect; it is the reversal of the logical to the ontological (Borella).

AC: This is an illustration of what you have been saying since the beginning of our interviews: metaphysics leads to its own erasure because it takes us beyond the pure and simple conceptual.

BB: In more technical terms, Jean Borella speaks of the irreducible semanticity of intellective consciousness. That is to say, meaning is received in the intelligence; it never creates it by itself.

This sense is that of reality, a degree of reality exceeding that in which it manifests itself. "The cognitive content of the intellect exceeds the degree of reality of its manifestation: in other words, it is transcendent to it," says Jean Borella.

AC: Here we rediscover Aristotle's saying that "the intellect comes through the door" or "from outside"; and above all we rediscover Plato and *noesis*: contemplation of essences.

BB: Perhaps even *gnosis*.

Chapter 4
Metaphysics and Esotericism

Briefly stated, with esotericism defined as a "revelatory" veil, and metaphysics as an unveiling through the "transparency of the intellect," this succinct definition of esotericism is deserving of further development. Hence the theme of this interview.

AC: During a previous interview, you briefly mentioned this distinction between esotericism and metaphysics. Could we come back to it in more detail?

BB: Of course. We can begin by drawing up a panorama of what certain academics have called "esotericism."

Esotericism, a brief inventory

Esotericism is certainly not absent from protohistoric eras, as for example the remains of megaliths bear witness, but even just over the past 2,500 years, several hundred esotericisms can be identified. Here are a few examples: the Orphism and Pythagoreanism of pre-Christian antiquity, the *Hermetica* (Alexandrian Hermeticism with the legendary Hermes Trismegistus), Neopythagoreanism, "gnosis" (Clement of Alexandria, 160–215; Origen, 185–254) and the Gnosticisms, the Manichaean current (third century), which will be found in Bulgarian Bogomilism (tenth century) then in Catharism (twelfth century), Neoplatonism followed by the Dionysian tradition, the *Sepher Yetsirah* of the fifth or sixth centuries, prefiguring medieval Kabbalah, visionary and spiritual alchemy (fourth to seventh century), the three great works of the ninth century: The *Book of the Secrets of Creation* (about 825) with a first version of the Emerald Tablet, the *Periphyseon* (about 865) by John the Scot, and the Arabic Epistles (ninth to tenth century) by the Brothers of Sincerity…

AC: Please, don't toss in any more!

BB: We can stop at this tenth-century date, but we have to acknowledge that there will be still more esotericisms from then until our days. Let us mention at least St Bonaventure, about whom we spoke earlier, with his "coincidence of opposites" heralding that of Nicholas of Cusa (1401–1464), who, with the idea of the fundamental unity of religions (*De pace fidei*, 1453) heralds the hermeticism of the Renaissance and, incidentally, the perennialism of the twentieth century. And the latter, by its criticism of the modern world and its doctrines of the convergence of religions, will have aided and abetted our New Age contemporaries.

AC: With esotericism, I rather had in mind initiatory organizations, or even schools around a spiritual master…

BB: There is, of course, Freemasonry, for example, which appeared in the sixteenth century in Scotland, but this is far from being the general case, as we have seen in the cited examples.

AC: I also see listed some fathers of the Church (Clement of Alexandria, Origen) or doctors of the Church (St Bonaventure). Is this not then theology?

BB: This is a real question, including for the scholars who have carried out these censuses (A. Faivre, for example). Classifying heresies as being "esoteric" is obvious, but an "approved" theology, however esoteric it may be, cannot, in my opinion, be an esotericism.

Esoteric or esotericism?

AC: Is there a difference between the esoteric and esotericism?

BB: In fact, I see a very big difference. "Esoteric" is a word that has existed since at least Antiquity, and means etymologically a movement "more inward than," that is to say, a knowledge that deepens more and more. On the other hand, "esotericism" is a recent word (nineteenth century), which refers to something composed: a system, an organization…

AC: In the passage from the adjective to the noun, the notion of movement is lost!

BB: And this is a problem. This noun has led to its complement: "exotericism" and both have been applied to religions, according to a somewhat crude schematism, in terms of duly constituted groups: Sufism as the esotericism of Islam, Taoism vis-à-vis Confucianism, Kabbalah for Judaism, Mahayana Buddhism versus Theravada.

AC: And in Christianity?

BB: Precisely the question! There is no such duly constituted organization, and to say that the discipline of the arcana of Christianity of the first centuries was an esotericism does not seem fair.

AC: Why is that?

BB: It was a question of not proceeding publicly with the administration of the sacraments (baptism, confirmation, eucharist), especially because of the persecutions. It should rather be said that Christianity has been, since then at least, both an integral esotericism (in the sense that the deepest mysteries are offered to all) or an integral exotericism (in the sense that all mysteries are offered to all). In other words, this esotericism-exotericism distinction makes little sense in characterizing a non-existent dividing-line within the Church.

AC: But then, what about this book the *Introduction to Christian Esotericism* that you mentioned?

BB: In fact, it is indeed the meaning of the adjective that must be seen there: what is involved here is a making known of the properly esoteric dimension of Christian dogmatics; it is even rather, formally, a *metaphysics of the Christian mysteries*. And of course, not through metaphysical concepts that would be applied to them, but, directly, a metaphysical explanation of what they contain and what they refer to for those who want to take the trouble to go deeper.

Esotericism and metaphysics

AC: So here is where metaphysics appears to have a sense that seems close to that of "esoteric."

BB: In this case, they prove to be complementary: "esoteric" invites deepening; "metaphysical" reveals the ultimate possible interpretation.

AC: This is the keyword: "interpretation," behind which esotericism and metaphysics can be placed, right?

BB: Not quite! Interpretations are more or less exoteric ("outside") or esoteric ("inside"), depending on the symbols or analogies employed. Yet the metaphysical interpretation is anchored in the language of intelligence (intuition of reality) that characterizes it. One could say that the interpretations found in the esotericisms are, rather, *rationally* constituted systems or doctrines, while the metaphysical interpretation fades away as soon as it has brought the *intelligence* to the reality to be contemplated.

AC: So metaphysics opens us to knowledge by participation, compared to knowledge by abstraction, as you indicated earlier. But reading symbols is common to both, right?

BB: This all depends, of course, on how the symbols are read. There are also more or less radical, more or less directly metaphysical symbolisms.

AC: Any examples?

BB: There are symbolisms of flowers, dreams, animals, shapes, metals, numbers, etc., which can be part of particular esotericisms, and other symbolisms, especially metaphysical, such as the symbol of the cross, which directly leads to a metaphysical understanding—e.g., the vertical is a link to the cause and to eternity, while the horizontal is bound up with human time and limits of all kinds. This reminds us that the On-High is not at the end of any "forging ahead."

AC: How then are we to define esotericism?

BB: As we have seen in the examples given, neither the notions of secret (the arcane), of hidden (the occult), of closure (hermeticism), of interior (esotericism), of initiation, or transmission, allow it to be defined. So many counterexamples accumulate each time! Yet it remains interesting to speak about systems of interpretation (of hermeneutics, in scholarly language). Interpretation is common to all science, to all knowledge, but here there arises the issue of fixing a border between interpretation and over-interpretation, as well as this necessary distinction between knowledge by abstraction and by participation.

Already, we can exclude occultism from esotericism.

AC: On what criteria?

BB: The former deals with cosmological forces, with magic; the latter all have a spiritual perspective, at least of the "angelic" type—let's say, of the intermediate worlds between man and God.

AC: Esotericisms are therefore relative to religions, whether orthodox or heterodox?

BB: We can say that, I think. Someone did propose as a general definition: "the hermeneutics of a symbolism and the tradition of this hermeneutics." (J.-P. Laurant)

AC: But what then is the value of symbolic knowledge? And what reality does a symbol have?

BB: Metaphysically, we must agree, with Plato, that the world is "of all necessity the image [the symbol] of something" (*Timaeus*, 29b). If, on the other hand, it was necessary, with Aristotle, to consider that the world is entirely *there*, that it suffices to measure it to know it, the symbol no longer has any possible reality.

AC: Indeed!

BB: Esotericism, at the very least, considers something beyond nature (the supernatural) or beyond the physical (the metaphysical). If we do not grant any reality to these "beyonds," esotericisms reduce to various lucubrations that can be stored in a sort of cabinet of curiosities.

On the other hand, if a reality is granted to these

"beyonds," it remains to be seen where this esoteric knowledge leads us.

AC: I understand. Is it an accumulation of "intermediary knowledge"? Does esotericism present itself as an end in itself? Or is it a provisional knowledge of intermediary realities allowing one to then approach "Reality" according to a mode of knowledge by participation?

BB: This is for me the decisive criterion. The question is: is this esotericism esoteric? That is to say, is it moving towards knowledge by participation or not?

AC: Metaphysics is definitely the final arbiter in this matter of esotericism. But isn't this the tool of discrimination used by the "codifier of esotericism" (Guénon)?

PART II

Personal Metaphysics

Chapter 5
Metaphysical Biography

This interview took place after several sessions, when I realized that to become a metaphysician one had to find roots in lived experience. It has also been said that "every metaphysical question involves the metaphysician who poses it" (Heidegger). I therefore asked a few personal questions of Bruno Bérard.

AC: Given the personal nature of any true entry into philosophy, I would like to ask you some questions of a personal nature. What in life makes one become a philosopher? How do you become a metaphysician?

BB: First of all, it must be made abundantly clear that I cannot say that I am a philosopher or a metaphysician. I am not a professional, a professor of these disciplines. Those who are called metaphysicians are, among others, Plato and Aristotle for Antiquity, Descartes and Leibniz for the modern era, and Guénon, Schuon, and Borella in the twentieth century.

AC: Are they so few?

BB: This is of course a selection, and we can add some fine names like Plotinus, St Thomas Aquinas, St Bonaventure, Meister Eckhart, Bergson, Blondel, Heidegger (in some way), and, under other skies (those of Islam, India, China, Japan): Lao Tzu, Nagarjuna, Shankara, Dogen, Al-Farabi, Avicenna, Averroes, Ibn Arabi, Kukai, Kitaro Nishida. And we could add as well all who have partially dealt with it…

AC: Let's get back then to this "metaphysical biography." If you are neither a philosopher nor a metaphysician, what about all your books on metaphysics?

BB: In fact, I readily admit to being a philosopher and a metaphysician, but like everyone else who tries to "think ahead." Anyway, "man is a metaphysical animal," said Schopenhauer.

AC: So, tell me when you became aware of it, when you started thinking like a philosopher, like a metaphysician.

BB: It is true that several events marked me, and marked me so well that I still remember them and have kept them in mind until today.

AC: Traumas are integral to identity, as Boris Cyrulnik (1937–) says...

Words and thought

BB: Certainly, even though "trauma" would be excessive in my case! Among these events, one of the most fundamental was, at the age of seven, my entry into the scouts. I had the image of righteousness, honesty, and daily good deeds. On the first day, on the occasion of a game (a search for a treasure hidden by the other team), I wanted to check on this uprightness by offering money to a member of the opposing team so that he would tell me the location of the treasure (I didn't have any money anyway). I was of course immediately convinced of his uprightness because of his great surprise and his refusal. It was when, later, the leader asked me what had come over me that I realized I was the one who had missed out on the word "upright." All I could say was that "it was to see if he was nice," when I was really thinking: "it was to check on his uprightness." I then

64

became aware of the usefulness of words to express one's thoughts, which is banal, but, above all, that thought goes beyond words.

AC: That is to say…?

BB: That is to say that there is on one side the contemplation of Ideas: this is Plato posing once and for all the possibility of metaphysical knowledge, and on the other, the expression of ideas with words: this is then Aristotle posing once and for all the rigor of scientific discourse.

AC: So there is science on one side and speculation on the other?

BB: Actually, not at all! It should immediately be clarified that "speculation" does not only have the pejorative meaning of "lucubration" sometimes given to it; the word comes from the Latin *speculum*, which means "mirror," that is to say that the Ideas are mirrored in us, we receive them by reflecting them.

Above all, there is no choice: the human mind allows both and needs both. One of these faculties has long been called reason: enabling scientific discourse and reasoning; the other, intelligence or intellect: enabling one to understand the reasoning, which otherwise is a simple logical or mechanical calculation. We cannot force ourselves to understand what we do not understand, said Simone Weil (1909–1943).

AC: I understand, but how is this a metaphysical experience?

BB: All the possibility of metaphysics is there. If there were no receiver in man to reflect what is beyond the physical world (the metaphysical) or what is beyond nature (the supernatural), metaphysics would be impossible. To put it Platonically: we could not participate in Ideas. At best, we would develop concepts, we would build, or even, we would only imagine what goes beyond the world.

AC: All right. And are there other events like this?

BB: First, there was this little sequel on words, when, at fourteen, on a ski course, some older students had fun calling those who did not know this vocabulary "scatophagical nymphomaniacs." It was, I must admit, a little frustrating, but an opportunity to understand the importance of using right and precise words and, above all, that words are used to communicate. This is again quite commonplace, but, then again, talking about metaphysics without philosophical jargon is precisely a challenge in these interviews.

AC: This is indeed our goal. So, to further clarify, can you specify how you see the relationship between words and thought?

BB: I believe there is the following dialectic: you think and then find the right word to express your thought in the most precise way (this was my experience, by default, on the first day at the scouts); at the same time, the words we learn (with the notions or concepts they convey) make it possible to refine or even deploy our thinking (the experience at the ski course). But thought will always go beyond words, it cannot be reduced to the language that can be used to express it. A rational and logical thought, which is based on reason, reduces thought to this rational construction as compared to an intuitive or participative thought of Ideas, which is intellectual intuition. Poetry allows you to experience it.

AC: But with poetry we are in the realm of emotion.

BB: In part, certainly, but this emotion is the counterpart of what is perceived intellectually and what is between the lines and beyond the words. To take it in another way, there are two ways to stop thinking: action or contemplation (Borella).

AC: Could you elaborate on that?

BB: In one case, having thought about something, it is implemented; in the other, one's thinking is led to go beyond words (or the concepts that words represent) and participate in the Idea that they designate. Typically, in one case we have the rational knowledge of modern science, which is realized through technical means; in the other we have metaphysical knowledge, which is realized through contemplation, that is, access to that which words and associated concepts designate.

AC: But, a physicist, for example, also accesses what the concepts of physics mean.

BB: Absolutely. The two instances of reason and intelligence are common to all people and to all activities. The main point, the metaphysical experience, is simply the recognition of the fact of intellectual intuition. To this intellectual intuition corresponds the existence of meaning, of signification, of significance (Borella), and this cannot be generated—meaning is not created, it is given. We "understand" because we encounter a meaning and we have the "mirror" of intelligence to recognize it. This is not quite the famous reminiscence of Plato. His doctrine deduces that we can only know new things by remembering, whereas here we only say that we know these new things because we are endowed beforehand with the adequate tool. The common point is in this "priorness." "You wouldn't be looking for me if you hadn't already found me," wrote Pascal (1623–1662), after Bernard of Clairvaux (1090–1153).

The others, the alter egos

AC: You wanted to mention another "metaphysical" event in your life?

BB: Yes, this other event that marked me deeply is also double: when I was about five years old and then about twelve. My earliest memory whatsoever is from about the age of five. At that time, although I was close to my mother and grandmother, I remember suddenly, at the entrance to our apartment in Nancy where we lived at the time, coming to an abrupt halt—for the first time I became aware of my father's actual existence. He had been with us all along in the rounds of our daily life, but, at that moment, I said to myself: "It is true, he does exist. I will have to take care of him." In my memory, it was really a question of correcting an oversight; in fact, it was my emergence out of a feminine and mothering cocoon, and my first look at other people.

AC: And your metaphysical interpretation?

BB: Clearly, this was a basic understanding for such a young age, but an obvious psychological interpretation would not do it justice and would be rather trite. Metaphysically, this event was, I believe, the discovery that one is not alone, nor at the center, but one among others. There appeared in me this mystery of the multiplicity of beings facing the unity of being. Of course, although I experienced it that way at the time, I did not think of it as such.

However, the question of individual destiny vis-à-vis a collective destiny of humanity has long preoccupied me. We will surely come back to that question.

AC: And your experience at twelve years?

BB: It was then, at the dawn of adolescence, that I began to look at adults with a critical eye. I found the way they all embraced their social persona to be quite ridiculous. Even beyond their function, I saw a particular doctor playing his character, the same for a particular policeman, a professor, an uncle, a salesman in a store, a politician... All authenticity had disappeared, all solidity. It even seemed to me that these role-playing characters gave them permission for any lack of kindness, or even wickedness. Such is the image we have of that Nazi torturer, who is only obeying orders; so it's not his fault! The character, the role, thus allows irresponsibility. In me, the unease was such that I began to pray morning and evening never to become an "idiot like an adult." This lasted a few years. I remember then, "waking up" from this state at around the age of seventeen (after having unfortunately forgotten to say these prayers for a while), I could say to myself: "Phew, it worked! It's up to me never to play a character and to always be kind, benevolent."

AC: And you were able to have an adult life on this basis?

BB: I got through it, but of course it hampered me in my professional career in industrial groups. A study has also been published showing that in general the most asocial people rise to the head of large companies...

AC: And the metaphysical interpretation?

BB: Very simple and completing the experience when five

years old! That is: behind the existence of multiple others, beyond the characters played, hides a deep bond, a relative identity among all, a metaphysical solidarity. We can call such solidarity love. This is the metaphysical bond *par excellence*, which all other bonds approach more or less closely…

What professional life?

AC: This will surely be a point to come back to. But, to continue this interview, could you say more about your life, both professional and "metaphysical," now that you are reaching retirement age?

BB: Yes. The three primary characteristics of my main professional activity have been: first, the chance to work all over the world and encounter many cultures; then, to be active in the context of stimulating and complex industrial activities of a scientific nature; and finally, to come into management positions specializing in strategy and corporate finance.

However, as "intelligent" as this professional activity may have been, and even sometimes associated with teaching, it was never enough for me. And so, early on, at around the age of twenty, I had begun studying metaphysics, then started writing a book that was eventually published when I was forty-seven. Already at age twenty I had wanted to describe the world and life synthetically and to share it with others. Today, at sixty-three, I understand that I have ended up being better qualified to do so, and I am delighted with the timing of these interviews. They must allow us to get to the point and share it in plain language—I hope!

AC: You said: "main professional activity," so there are others?

BB: Indeed. I was lucky that my first two books were published by L'Harmattan. I also facilitated the transfer to L'Harmattan of the Delphica series from L'Âge d'Homme, which became the *Théôria* series, in which I have been collaborating since. At the same time, the director of L'Harmattan, Denis Pryen, encouraged me to set up a series there. Of course, I seized this opportunity and created a series on metaphysics, of which the first title to be published was *Souvenirs métaphysiques d'Orient et d'Occident*, by François Chenique. I wanted this collection to bring together real-life or illustrative metaphysical texts, dialogues, collections on subjects such as What is Metaphysics? Metaphysics and Psychoanalysis, Physics and Metaphysics, Metaphysics of Fairy Tales… I wanted to call this series "La métaphysique apprivoisée" ("Metaphysics Tamed"), but L'Harmattan opted for "Métaphysique au quotidien" ("Everyday Metaphysics").

AC: And can we say that this series is doing well?

BB: For its size, it is acceptable, and we have been able to publish about fifteen books in twelve years.

I was also professionally occupied for about a dozen years with strategic and merger-acquisition consulting, particularly in the aerospace and defense industries. I was quite active during those years, for example, with Boeing.

AC: You just can't stop yourself, can you (laughs)? That's quite a few lines of work! As for your entry into metaphysics prior to the publishing opportunity at L'Harmattan, I imagine significant personal encounters played a role?

Four significant encounters

BB: Absolutely. These meetings were fundamental; you

don't do anything all alone! I won't mention the decisive professional encounters from which I have benefited, but limit myself to those related to metaphysics. In this area, where we can say that everything has already been said, it therefore remains to say it differently, as best we can. There, encounters with people or books are real keys: they throw open doors in the mind. These people were my father Pamphile, Lanza del Vasto, François Chenique, and Jean Borella.

AC: Can you say a few words about each?

BB: Of course! I was lucky to have a father who was both educated in multiple disciplines (mathematics, astrology, physics, dietetics, philosophy, yoga, botany, theology, etc.), having attended major seminary before getting married, having contributed to the development of yoga in France (for a time president of the French Federation), teaching Eastern philosophy (vedanta, samkhya)—all the while working as an engineer in the social services of the Charbonnages de France (national coal industry) and, not to forget, publishing numerous books (including an award by the French Academy for a book of poetry, *Le fil des Êtres*, 1967).

AC: Impressive!

BB: But there is still more! He called himself Pamphile, that is to say "one who loves everything," and his reputation for kindness, benevolence, understanding of others was beyond compare. He quoted Baden-Powell, founder of the scouts, abridging the complete motto, "in every boy, there is at least 5% of good. It is up to you to discover it and to develop it up to 90 or 95%,"to: "in every man, there is at least 5% of good" and towards everyone, including his two children, he had in mind only this 5%. It was, of course, a positive pedagogy, by example and through trust, in which our mother was always involved.

AC: What more could you wish for? And what do you owe him more precisely?

BB: I will mention three of his contributions to my education, just to keep things short (laughs). How exasperating he seemed to me when I was a teenager. He seemed so naive in his dealings with businessmen and tradespeople, but his "kindness" ended up being a model for relationships with others, and I see that my sister followed this same pattern and espoused the same attitude. All in all, this "kindness" is very closely related to what Christianity calls charity, and Buddhism or Islam calls compassion. In metaphysics, whether Christian or Hindu, we have the paths of union with the "absolute" through knowledge (the intellect as a kind of "way of approach") and through love (devotion). But of course they converge to become only one. Without the love of wisdom or the wisdom of love (philosophy), one does not go far.

His second contribution involved the craft of writing, whether this had to do with expressing oneself clearly and in the right sequence, or with poetry. I recall being assigned an essay for homework, a deeply frustrating task. To my surprise, while I stood there beside my father watching, he wrote it all out for me from start to finish! This was the lesson received at twelve that would serve me all my life.

AC: And did you get a good grade? (laughs).

BB: Yes, *he* got a good grade, but, above all, from that day on, I was freed up by this example, and able to progress from there.

The third contribution concerns religions. Strongly into the principle of a human tripartition (but which I do not remember him ever mentioning specifically): body, psyche, spirit, he opened me to religion. He thought, with regard to education, that children need conditioning, but that it is then necessary to provide them with the bases of their own deconditioning. Thus, he said: "just as one cannot leave children without language, in order that they can choose later in which language they might wish to express themselves, it is also advisable to endow them with a religion, but in a way that does not exclude others." With a Catholic background, he nevertheless opened me up in particular to Orthodoxy and the religions of India, whose metaphysics he taught.

AC: Here we have this relationship between metaphysics, or more generally philosophy, and religions, of which we spoke earlier. So let's move on to Lanza del Vasto, disciple of Gandhi (1869–1948) and founder of the L'Arche communities. It is not trivial to meet such a character.

BB: I have been very lucky. At the time I was perhaps ten years old (it was at the end of the Sixties), but I saw him at least twice, with his wife Chanterelle, when they came home for dinner. Lanza wanted our family to join some L'Arche community. I did not have a conversation with him that I remember, but he is one of those people whose mere presence teaches. Subsequently, reading his biography (he died in 1981) or his books, I saw nothing but the transparency of his person.

AC: What do you mean by "transparency"?

BB: Let's say, authenticity and veracity; a person, precisely, without character, if you will. And that is also one of the objects of prayers he had composed: the "Rappel" ("Reminder"), to help us remember we are not our thoughts, our character, our body, etc.

AC: We have two outstanding encounters left to discuss, François Chenique and Jean Borella...

BB: It's good to talk about them together because both lived in Nancy until the early 1970s; they and my father were three friends—and remained so until the end (François died in 2012, my father in 2019). It was on the occasion of my first book, which integrated a significant part of their respective works, that I was able to have metaphysical discussions with them.

The first contact was somewhat delicate, because my text often quoted them without quotation marks and without references.

AC: How is it possible?

BB: I wanted to have their opinion on a draft, that is, logically arranged reading notes for a future book; naturally, the finished book was done according to the rules of the art. Above all, after pleading my case, I was able to obtain a critical afterword from Jean Borella to this first book, then to publish books from both of them.

AC: And what about those relationships?

BB: These are relationships of friendship; they honor me particularly, given the admiration I have for them. François spoke seven languages, including Sanskrit and Tibetan, which enabled him to make cross-translations of great texts of Buddhism, and I had for years as a bedside book his treatise on classical logic, which, by the way, I had reissued by L'Harmattan. I found him to have an intelligence *à la* St

Thomas Aquinas—which is not nothing (and probably too much). His logical and synthetic way of exposition makes many of his texts masterpieces. But like any true scientist, he knew how to say "I don't know." For example, I asked him once how individual and collective perspectives were coordinated after death, but, this time, I only heard a sigh of helplessness. And I remember the regret he expressed, shortly before his death, for having worked too much.

AC: Roger Bacon (1214–1294) too said: "I repent of having taken so much trouble in the interest of science."

BB: I see this as analogous to what St Thomas Aquinas himself said, shortly before his death, in speaking of his work—both considerable and unequaled—that it was straw compared to a vision he had during a religious service. I also have taken this to heart: not to sacrifice life and family to a science, even metaphysics, and to remember that metaphysics itself should not be a goal, it being rather a path.

As for Jean, I would say that I was struck, when reading his books, by such an understanding that I had the distinct impression of writing them as I read them. For me, it was always the right questions, the right answers, and in the right order. When I next met him (on the occasion of my first book), I was comforted by his benevolence and encouragement. One of the main points of his teaching to me comes from our first interview. In essence, he told me: "one should not try too hard to affirm in a categorical way; things are aporetic, that is to say problematic, and may contain insoluble contradictions, so schematics are useful, but dangerous; you can use them initially, but then have to go beyond them."

Today I see how this applies to the relatively artificial categories of esotericisms and exotericisms, and above all (as we said at the beginning of this interview) to the fact that the role of metaphysics is to take us beyond words and speech to the contemplation of pure reality. As for the contradictions, which are found as far as the mode of knowing, this gave rise to my *Metaphysics of Paradox*, begun in 2007 and published in 2019.

There were of course many other encounters, whether person or book, each shedding light on one point or another, refining one position or another, but, once you get started, these things flesh out or deepen thought more than they alter it or modify it profoundly. Anyway, that's my experience.

Initiation, initiation books

AC: I have one last question, perhaps even more personal. Do you need an initiation to enter metaphysics?

BB: No, every human being is more or less a metaphysician. That said, I believe initiation can be understood, and from several points of view. There is a text on the question, cowritten by Pamphile, Chenique, and Borella, published in the *Revue française de yoga*, but I don't remember it precisely. The most traditional point of view is the initiation one receives from a master following an unbroken chain of transmission in religions or in certain societies, sometimes secret: ancient (the mystery cults of Egypt or Greece) or more modern (for example the Compagnonnages or Freemasonry, which practice rites of passage and appeared in the sixteenth century in Scotland). In primitive Christianity, this was the case with the *sacraments* of initiation (baptism, confirmation, and the Eucharist) and communicated in secret (law of the arcana) for protection against persecution—but they have now been public for a very long time and the details of the rituals and results of the initiations are known to all, or at least available in full in theological treatises.

For my part, and as far as metaphysics is concerned, I have no "initiations" to tally up. There were those of my father speaking to me about Vedanta, giving me books by Guénon, and giving me an initiation name: *tatdas*, a Sanskrit word meaning servant (*das*) of the absolute (*tat*). I have never mentioned this publicly.

AC: Why not?

BB: Contrary to what was still common practice at the beginning of the twentieth century, my era was no longer that of pseudonyms. It was François Chenique who discouraged me from using it or letting my first book be anonymous. Also, I found that this name pertained to the private domain. If I mention it today, it is because I believe it helped me remain, precisely, a "servant"—that is, in the service of others as far as possible. Finally, bearing witness to this without hiding anything is not always without use for others: "what is most personal is perhaps the most universal." (Henri Nouwen, 1932–1996)

Alongside Catholicism, Orthodoxy, Vedanta, Guénon, and even the Kabbalah, Sufism, and Taoism—of course I am not putting everything on the same level, far from it—I believe I took an (intellectual) turn when reading three authors: Father Stéphane, a priest theologian and metaphysician of the twentieth century (it was François Chenique who had ensured the publication by Dervy of his *Introduction to Christian Esotericism*), St Dionysius the Areopagite, and Meister Eckhart, with many key elements that I found later and with many other things in Borella's work.

AC: With a priest, St Dionysius the Areopagite, and Meister Eckhart, are we still in metaphysics then, or have we moved into religion?

BB: These "domains" are very distinct, one as a science, the other as a confession, but they have two fundamental points in common. First, there is the metaphysical; this will be called "Unmoved Mover," First Principle, etc., in metaphysics and, quite simply, God, in religion. The second common point, just as central, and which can be a source of confusion, is the metaphysical language, that is to say the ultimate interpretations and formulations of what is revealed to the metaphysical intelligence. Even though some metaphysicians, such as Heidegger, dissociate themselves from their religion, the greatest theologians develop a metaphysical discourse on the dogmatics (the formulation of the "mysteries") of their confession, such as most of the Fathers and Doctors of the Church.

There is, therefore, a metaphysical language that can be adapted to a religion (incorporating the Platonic and Aristotelian resonances we find in Christianity; and, more directly, the metaphysics of the Christian mysteries, which theologians will know how to formulate.

AC: This is quite clear, and of course the interview "Metaphysics and Religion" has already somewhat elaborated on this question.

Chapter 6

An Adventure into Metaphysics

After having considered "metaphysical journey" as the title for this chapter, I opted for "adventure," with the feeling that, when one engages in metaphysics, when one undertakes this journey, one cannot know in advance what to expect. The idea adopted here is to follow the chronology of Bruno's various published works, while benefiting at the same time from a synthetic presentation of each.

AC: I would like to suggest that you illustrate your "adventure" in metaphysics by following the chronology of your published books.

BB: Why not, with this reservation that the writing periods do not always correspond to the publication dates.

Introduction à une métaphysique des mystères chrétiens (2005); *A Metaphysics of the Christian Mystery* (2018); *Introduzione a una metafisica cristiana* (2021)

This first book was the result of twenty years of reading a multitude of philosophical, esoteric, metaphysical, and theological works concerning six religions: Buddhism, Christianity, Hinduism, Islam, Judaism, and Taoism. When I started to write it, I had just discovered Father Stéphane (*"Introduction to Christian Esotericism"*), François Chenique (*The Burning Bush*), and Jean Borella (*Love and Truth* [*The Desecration of Charity*, in its first edition], as well as *Guénonian Esotericism and Christian Mystery*). Being a

Catholic with forays into Orthodoxy, I knew enough about Christian theology to recognize how powerful the corresponding metaphysical formulations could be. This explains why this first book, rather than setting out a comparison of religions, was centered on three Christian mysteries: the Trinity, the Virgin, and Christ—the elements from other religions giving the subtitle: "with regard to Buddhist, Hindu, Islamic, Judaic, and Taoist traditions." As the bishop who was kind enough to preface it (Mgr Dubost) wrote: "the elements of other religions come into harmonious resonance with the Christian elements, and each religion is in a way enlightened by the others, each retaining its own identity."

AC: We are far from a single metaphysical discourse unifying all religions and risking, in a way, reducing them to their lowest common denominator. How is it that this book received the *imprimatur* of the Catholic Church?

BB: Having no particular authority and speaking of Christian theology, I absolutely wanted the text to be verified. This is why I went to find François Chenique, Jean Borella, and the Catholic Institute of Paris, whose dean referred me to the *imprimatur* office of the diocese of Paris.

AC: And did many things have to be modified?

BB: I remember two things. The priest who gave the initial *nihil obstat* (that is to say "no obstacle") had been a missionary in Africa, where he was faced with great poverty; so, he asked me to attenuate certain formulas of Father Stéphane about the "poverty" of the divine persons. He also asked me to suppress the notion of a "co-redeeming Mary," which I had taken from Chenique, but which, in the meantime, had been cautiously withdrawn by the Church (there is one Redeemer only: Christ), even though this subject is still under discussion. But that would take us too far!

I wanted to make it a simple book, unburdened with footnotes, and offering the reader, for each mystery, several approaches: conceptual, theological, mysterial, metaphysical, and esoteric—this is where the analogies between religions transpire—and each part closing with striking texts allowing meditation, even contemplation, of the mystery.

AC: Does it contain something more than other similar works?

BB: Apart from the fact that Jean Borella noted in his afterword that this book is unprecedented, I would just like to emphasize this idea of a "two-step cure," with a first stage left to man's freedom and the second left to the bounty of God. These two steps are identified in the seven traditions (for instance, a Lesser Vehicle and Great Vehicle are distinguished in Buddhism, to make it seven in all). This could be placed in an appendix.

Also original with the book was, I believe, the presentation of the Christian mysteries in the form of numerous paradoxes along with the discovery that, for the highest paradoxes, the truth appears closest at hand.

AC: An example of these paradoxes?

BB: One God in three persons, true man and true God, immanence and transcendence. And there are many others.

AC: With, by now, nearly twenty years of hindsight, what do you think of this book?

BB: Basically, I find there is nothing to amend and this is why versions have recently been published in the United States (*A Metaphysics of the Christian Mystery*, Angelico

Press, 2018) and in Italy (*Introduzione a una metafisica cristiana*, Simmetria, 2021). As to its form, I would try to rewrite it even more simply for a wider audience. I would also add a fourth part on the Holy Spirit, which is really missing. "We always have an interest in praying to the Holy Spirit, if I may say so," Jean Borella confided to me one day. I am convinced of that today. He is the one who "bloweth where [He] listeth" (John 3:8) and who "maketh intercession for us with unutterable groanings" (Rom 8:26). We could talk about this in the context of an interview on the creation of the world...

Jean Borella, The Metaphysical Revolution (2006)

There are several good reasons for this second book. The main one is that, after the first book, I had the feeling of having gone to the end of what we could know and of contemplating the eternal truths, dare I say.

AC: To this point?

BB: Absolutely, and it is still the case today. I live every day in the sublime atmosphere of the Christian mysteries, which I have approached once and for all, as it seems to me. On the other hand, on a philosophical level, I had a lot of catching up to do. Since I had submitted to Jean Borella a synthetic summary of one of his books, and he had thought well of it, I undertook to summarize all his works to date according to theme.

It took me a colossal amount of work at night, on weekends, and all the holidays to assimilate more than three thousand five hundred pages and to restore them synthetically in three hundred and fifty. But it served me as a kind of apprenticeship in philosophy and, it seems, a practical tool for readers of Borella.

AC: The following book, on the other hand, seems very personal.

Introduction à la métaphysique. Les trois songe (2008)

BB: Indeed. I wanted to start writing simpler books for the general public if possible, and thought it would facilitate understanding if the metaphysical interpretation related to concrete things: dreams, myths, fairy tales... Now, I had at my disposal dreams that I actually had. These gave rise to this little book, with a *crescendo* passing from the related dreams to the *grand finale* of metaphysics, if you will, that is to say the notion of the "Beyond of being"; passing through what an interpretation is, then the metaphysical interpretation of dreams, to end with a definition of metaphysics.

AC: If I may say so, I have read it, but do you think you might be able to simplify things even more?

BB: Yes, my goal is to accomplish that someday.

AC: It was then that you launched the idea of collective books.

Collective books

BB: Exactly. Having surveyed what I could understand and give back at this stage, the idea of collective books came to me, the idea being, on the one hand, to deal metaphysically with subjects that I was not able to fully master, and on the other to offer multiple points of view on the same question, with a resulting wealth of insights.

Qu'est-ce que la métaphysique? ("What is Metaphysics?" 2010). I had the chance to bring together twelve authors, including Pamphile, Wolfgang Smith, Chenique, and

Borella, and by this means was able to show that if meta-physics does not stand in the void, this is not only because it involves the metaphysician who thinks it, but also because it applies to all the things of the world, thought, and life. Permit me to add here an excerpt from my introduction to the book:

> Thus, metaphysics, according to each contributor to this book, is related to its practice, to art, politics, and poetry, to its recent rediscovery of analogy, to logic, the outer boundary of which it is, to the Christian doctrine of creation *ex nihilo*, to physics, phenomenology and mysticism, to its possibility in Buddhism, to every dogmatic doctrine that would affirm truth as well as doubt, and to the history of its name and its concept as far as the possibility of any act of knowing.

AC: Nice program! many readers?

BB: I haven't checked recently, but I'd say several hundred, which corresponds pretty well to the readership for this type of work.

Métaphysique des contes de fées (*The Metaphysics of Fairy Tales*, 2011). Co-written with Jean Borella, I am delighted with this book. It forced me to attempt a metaphysical interpretation of a fairy tale (by Andersen), and Borella himself offered brilliant metaphysical comments on two tales (by Perrault and Grimm).

Métaphysique et psychanalyse (*Metaphysics and Psychoanalysis*, 2013). This brought together six authors representing the one side or the other. With hindsight, and the limited number of copies sold, I believe that if metaphysical interpretation includes psychoanalysis, the latter rather simply denies metaphysics, ranking it among the phantasms of the unconsciousness. This is why it would perhaps have been better to publish a conversation between a metaphysician and a psychoanalyst, rather than simply recording opposing theses.

AC: There is now in preparation this book of interviews *Metaphysics for everyone*. Are there any others?

BB: There is a book on *Trends and Pitfalls of Esotericism*, in progress for several years with Jean-Pierre Brach, Aldo La Fata, Jean-Pierre Laurant; and another, *Christian Sayings, Misinterpretation, and Truth* with Aldo La Fata. Unfortunately, Jean Borella could no longer participate.

AC: What is the idea of this last book?

BB: Very simple: to offer a selection of well-known formulas such as "judge not," "love and do what you want," "many are called, but few are chosen," "outside the Church, no salvation," etc., and comment on them by proposing the most relevant metaphysical interpretation.

AC: In the meantime, you have resumed writing several other books.

Metaphysics of Paradox (2019)

BB: I started this work on paradoxes in 2007, after discovering that the best knowledge of Christian mysteries stops at insoluble paradoxes and that it is then necessary to "jump into the void." But it is not only the rational knowledge of God that stops at paradoxes; it is the same as far as knowing the world, man, and society.

AC: Examples?

BB: In cosmology, we have a finite world, but without

boundaries; in physics, there is Schrödinger's cat, regarding whom we cannot know whether it is alive or dead. Concerning society: no one is supposed to ignore the law, but the law has become unknowable, according to the country's (France's) highest courts of appeal. And there are many more.

I wanted then to apply to paradoxes the philosophical method as developed in Jean Borella's book *Penser l'analogie* (*Thinking Analogy*).

AC: But can't one do metaphysics without recourse to philosophy and its methods?

BB: Partly. Metaphysics really requires the philosophical method on its rational side only, which is why at one time the three parts of academic metaphysics were called: rational cosmology, rational psychology, and rational theology. And so I wanted to learn how to apply the philosophical method to my thinking. Of course, I called for help from specialists at the École Pratique des Hautes Études, the Sorbonne and the Collège de France, but without success.

AC: What do you mean?

BB: I think these professors are so busy, that they can't even find the time to say they don't have time. It's a bit sad. I therefore undertook on my own to write this thesis regarding paradoxes, which consisted in showing that everything that is to be known comes up against paradoxes, but that there is a possible knowledge, itself paradoxical: metaphysics. Complementary to knowledge by analogy, there is thus knowledge by paradox. And just like the symbol, the paradox has an anagogic virtue.

AC: Anagogic?

BB: To ascend, to be carried upward, drawing the eye of the soul out of the quagmire, as Plato put it. Thus, the symbol leads to what it is only the image of, and is recognized as such. And similarly, the paradox obliges us to realize that reality is beyond it: it has a true metaphysical function; it even deserves a specific interview.

AC: Noted. And even as we speak I believe two of your books are in the works.

BB: Yes, but meanwhile there was the book on Lacuria.

Lacuria (2020)

Father Lacuria (1806–1890) was a nineteenth-century priest, theologian, and metaphysician. The study of his life and work constituted my doctoral thesis. Comparing a life and a work is very instructive: one has the impression of seeing what is going on in the mind of the writer.

Métaphysique du Sexe (2022)

BB: The first book, which comes out as we speak, is a metaphysics of sex.

AC: A book was also written on the subject by the Italian metaphysician Julius Evola (1898–1974), right?

BB: This is indeed the title of his 1958 book, but it doesn't really deal with metaphysics, except for the small chapter entitled "Metaphysics of Sex," where we find in truncated form the myth reported by Aristophanes and excerpted from Plato's *Symposium*. Above all, Evola explicitly renounces (in his introduction) metaphysics *per se* and in reality offers a book entirely devoted to sex as a transpsychological and transphysiological power, linked to his interest in "intermediate worlds" and magic.

AC: We are indeed far from metaphysics.

BB: Which does not detract from Julius Evola. He is a real metaphysician, as can be clearly seen through his other works.

As far as a real metaphysics of sex is concerned, apart from my own approaches, there is little except what is to be found in the great Andalusian metaphysician Ibn 'Arabi (1165–1240) or in Jean Borella's masterpiece *Un homme une femme au paradis* [*A Man, A Woman, in Paradise*] (2008). Of course, I have integrated their work into my own.

AC: Was there not also *The Metaphysics of Sexual Love* (1818) by Schopenhauer?

BB: Yes, "sexual love" (*Geschlechtsliebe* in German), but the author sees only the species pole, that is, reproduction and speaks as well of sexual instinct, which is scientifically false. He is one of those celibate philosophers, like Heraclitus, Plato, Descartes, Spinoza, Leibniz, or even virgins like Nietzsche or Kant, who have been rather silent on this question of sex, except for a few errors like those committed by Kant or Schopenhauer (which of course does not detract from their genius in other matters).

La démocratie du future, le partage du pouvoir
[*The Future of Democracy, Power Sharing*] (2022)

The other book coming out at this time is about democracy.

AC: And what relationship with metaphysics?

BB: For a long time, I wondered why French presidents proclaimed "Long live the Republic!" and never "Long live democracy!" even though they make the latter the ultimate of any human society. Above all, how could they claim to identify democracy and representative government, which the American founders and French revolutionaries were careful not to do, since they opposed them.

It is, at the start of course, about political philosophy, but when we come to the notions of obedience, freedom, equality, and fraternity, metaphysics assumes its full rights and allows us to shed some light on this question of democracy. Anyway, that's what I thought. I started from societal paradoxes as identified in *Metaphysics of Paradox* and tried to show in three steps what a real democracy could be.

AC: Three steps?

BB: The democratic illusion, democratic impossibility, and democratic potentiality. It is indeed easy at first to show the incredible gap between the will of the citizens and the political decisions that are taken, between democratic principles and their implementation. That is the democratic illusion: a representation that does not represent, coupled with the oxymoron "representative democracy." Then come those elements that make any democracy impossible.

AC: Examples?

BB: One must know the law, but it is unknowable; the presumption of innocence is recognized, but the media freely and widely disseminate suspicions of guilt as soon as they arise; justice, supposed to be equal for all, allows itself to issue *exemplary* judgments, and we think of distributing the three powers (executive, legislative, judicial), but certain other powers seem above them: the media and economic considerations, for example.

Fortunately, there is a democratic potential. It is found at the heart of the original meaning of democracy, which is the sharing of power in time, in space, and in part in turn.

Hence the necessary renewal of democracy in "pancracy" (power belongs to everyone—but not at the same time!) or in "diacracy" (it is shared).

AC: But is this metaphysics?

BB: Yes, insofar as arriving at this conclusion, we are not only looking at the history or current events of current (pseudo-) democracies, but, as we said, are wondering about the metaphysics of society especially in terms of freedom, equality, and fraternity.

AC: All right. Finally, can you say a few words about your current projects?

BB: There are three main ones. First, there is a "Metaphysics of Relationship," as we evoked earlier in connection with the Trinity, but now applied to man, from his Creation to his eschatological destiny.

AC: Could you clarify man's eschatological destiny? Do you mean the destiny of a particular human being after death, or the destiny of humanity as a whole and of the universe at the end of time?

BB: I mean both aspects: the personal and the collective. In fact, much has been written on this theme in terms of the metaphysics of being, with the paradoxical coexistence of being and beings, of the One and the multiple—but behind this paradox I see a reality of a relational order, and therefore the need to formulate a metaphysics of relationship.

AC: But hasn't this already long since been done?

BB: Of course, as Jean Borella said not so long ago: "everything has already been said." From what I have seen so far, we find such elements in St Thomas Aquinas, in Lanza del Vasto, in Jean Borella... I certainly did not invent this subject; but it nonetheless remains, if I manage to do so, to offer a synthesis of this question.

Another project could be called "Metaphysics and Mysticism." This subject would lend itself well to a collective book.

AC: As for the third project in progress, I understand that it is a "Metaphysics of Believing"…

BB: Yes, with the idea of showing what remains in terms of knowledge at the bottom of that total ignorance in which man finds himself. Ultimately, the only thing we know is that we know nothing; which the great scholars have all admitted, from Plato to Max Planck. There is also this wonderful formula from Rachid Benzine: "the opposite of knowledge is not ignorance, but certainties." (*Lettres à Nour*) From this point of view, I would like to show this "kernel of gnosis" (Borella) that I believe is buried at the bottom of uncertainty.

AC: Nice program! I would now like to ask you one last crucial question. If, as you said, you "contemplated the eternal truths" while writing your first book, why all these studies and all the following books?

BB: There is one thing that makes them compatible: to be at the service of this contemplation and the irrepressible need to share it. Beyond that, whether or not I manage to transcribe these ideas clearly, whether there are many interested readers or not, is no longer up to me. I do what I think I should do, period.

AC: And to develop a marketing of metaphysics, obviously, would correspond to killing metaphysics. We will see if this "Metaphysics for Everyone" will be of great interest or not.

BB: Yes, we'll see. If we had to conclude on this idea of "metaphysical adventure," I would say there is none. I see life metaphysically, and all subjects lending themselves to it: sex, politics, paradox, relationships, psychoanalysis, physics… The subjects vary; the metaphysical perspective remains unchanged.

Chapter 7
Metaphysics and Metaphysicians

To understand how the various contributions to metaphysics can be so different as between a Plato and an Aristotle for example, one wonders if there is one metaphysics or several metaphysics. Thus, after having believed one has found the ultimate of things, one has the impression of falling back into the shreds and tatters of beliefs and opinions. The question had to be asked.

AC: With this capital difference between Plato and Aristotle, as you indicated, I wonder: is there is a metaphysics in the singular, or are there metaphysics in the plural. What do you think it is?

Metaphysics, material object and formal object

BB: As is often the case, you'll find everything, but, through the profusion of viewpoints it is possible to find your way. By its material object, if we follow St Thomas Aquinas, metaphysics is the science of everything that manifests the supernatural (God, soul, angels, etc.).

AC: Isn't that theology, then?

BB: Not at all: whereas theology has its source in revelation, metaphysics has its source in reason and intelligence. To put it simply, we have here both Plato and Aristotle. First: with intellectual intuition we have Plato, who will place his signature on a Neoplatonic (and Augustinian) Europe throughout the first millennium (and beyond, in waves). Second: having discovered Aristotle late in the Middle Ages, we see in it a science prior to Revelation, which however reaches the First Being, God, who is thus accessible to simple reason (forgetting the role of intellectual intuition). This double faculty constituted by reason and intelligence will fade later: first with Descartes, who confounds these two instances into one: a natural reason; then, above all, Kant, who deny all intellectual intuition, to the benefit of reason alone.

The material objects of metaphysics will vary over time and according to author. Some will speak of knowledge of the immaterial (Bossuet, 1627–1704); others will speak of the search for the Absolute, of knowledge of things in themselves (Schopenhauer, but then denying access to it, following Kant). Bergson (1859–1941) will speak of absolute knowledge by direct intuition, returning in this way to Plato.

AC: It is obvious to see to what extent all Western thought is tossed between rationalism and intellectual intuition, and this in reference to two philosophers who lived no less than 2,400 years ago!

BB: The positive aspect here is that Caesar is given back what belongs to him, and so for the most part I see intellectual honesty at work in philosophy. In any case, the material objects of metaphysics will have essentially remained "Being and beings" (*cf.* Blondel) and primary Being; or else, in more modern terms, being in itself and knowledge in itself. What will have changed is the question of the possibility of metaphysics. Quite simply, metaphysics becomes impossible if we deprive the human being of his fullness of mind and reduce him instead to his simple reason.

AC: I believe this is very clear as far as the material object of metaphysics is concerned, but what about in terms of formal object?

BB: If for a time metaphysics took on the meaning of critique of knowledge (this was prior to the development of philosophical or scientific epistemology), that is because it is a question of knowing *in reality and in truth*. The formal object is not some abstraction (most often a mathematical abstraction resulting from the process of reduction that is so integral to modern science); it is, rather, the already mentioned *participatory knowledge*. Concepts and symbols should allow truths to be realized *ontologically*, not just perceived *speculatively*. It is precisely in this sense that metaphysics constitutes a path. And that is why we can say that metaphysical truths can be approached according to the three traditional paths—those of action, love and knowledge, which is to say the hero, the saint and the sage. These paths correspond to the active, affective, and cognitive faculties of human nature (Chenique). We have here the obvious parallel with the three Hindu yogas: karma-yoga, bhakti-yoga and jñana-yoga. Each of these paths unfolds according to degrees, schematically reduced to three.

AC: An example?

BB: The three degrees of the path of knowledge that can be distinguished are the path of "study" or "science," the path of "speculative meditation," and the path of "contemplative concentration" (Schuon).

But these paths of heroism, wisdom, and holiness should not be seen as mutually exclusive. The path of knowledge and the path of love or devotion have sometimes been contrasted (in India: vicara-marga and bhakti-marga), but it has also been shown that they converge and become unified (Chenique). How, indeed, to love what one knows nothing about, and how to know completely what one does not love at all?

AC: I believe that the material and formal objects of metaphysics are quite clear. Can we illustrate them with the help of a presentation of some metaphysicians?

Some metaphysicians

BB: You might know that some great minds may, for example, have spent their entire lives studying Aristotle, but this is obviously not my case. In other words, what I am going to be able to say will necessarily be quite succinct and probably too schematic. But, let's try the exercise and start with Plato and Aristotle, even if we have already talked a lot about them.

PLATO. Plato appears to me as the actual founder of (Western) metaphysics. For him, to know is to know what is; however, nothing that we see—this stone, this tree, this cat...—is ever entirely there. The truth of knowledge will therefore be linked to the reality of its object, and there will be "degrees of knowledge corresponding rigorously to degrees of reality" (Borella). "Plato, for the first time in the history of philosophical thought, expressly applies the notion of analogy to the resolution of the most fundamental questions of metaphysics." (Borella) This is where the Platonic dialectic plays its full role: abandonment of discursive knowledge (*dianoïa*) and actualization of the intellect (*nous*). This is Plato's so-called *analogy of the line* (see Appendix I, page 157), and the famous text of the *Republic* (VII, 533d) should be cited, in which, thanks to this dialectical method, "the eye of the soul" is freed from the "barbaric quagmire" where it was buried:

> [I]s not dialectic the only process of inquiry that advances in this manner, doing away with hypotheses, up to the first principle itself in order to find confirmation there. And it is literally true that when the eye of the soul is sunk in a barbarous quagmire... dialectic gently draws it forth and leads it up.

AC: The poetry in Plato's style is notable.

BB: Yes, the knowledge attained by participation or contemplation is then more easily expressed in a pictorial or poetic way. This is why "theoretical discourse is the last resort for the teaching of truth" (*Letter* VII, 326a–b), as Plato has said.

AC: And this is where Aristotle, founder of the rigor of scientific discourse and logic, comes in—he, who is rather distant from poetry.

BB: Above all, he does not understand the existence of the world of Ideas, although he was Plato's pupil for 19 years. This is the death of all possibility of the symbol...

AC: That is to say...?

BB: The symbol: what *ontologically* connects a visible to an invisible. But, that said, there is indeed in Aristotle a supernaturalism of intelligible forms (when he says that "intelligence comes through the door").

ARISTOTLE. What he seeks above all is scientific certainty in the physical domain, that is to say a functioning of knowledge exclusively by abstraction. In his famous "the soul is *in a certain way* all that it knows" (*De Anima*), for example, a stone or a lion, "in a certain way" clearly indicates that the act of knowing completely separates being from intellect. This is why, on the contrary, because it is *entitatively* nothing of what it knows, the soul can *intentionally* identify itself with everything known. Knowledge then becomes a mere abstraction. It wrests from real and concrete being the intelligible form, thus allowing it to exist in the soul to which it unites by informing it. Such an "intelligible form is then nothing other than what is called a concept." Unfortunately, what is valid for the sensible world is not so for the intelligible world, which Aristotle denies (Borella).

AC: And yet Aristotle is a metaphysician?

BB: Yes, we owe him, in addition to his fourteen books on metaphysics still studied at the university twenty-four centuries later, this "scientific metaphysics" or, better said, this academic discipline that deals with being and principles with all the rigor of scientific discourse and without forgetting key metaphysical notions such as potentiality and its actuation—which we have already mentioned.

ST THOMAS AQUINAS. St Thomas Aquinas (1225/6–1274), known as the Angelic Doctor, wrote without doubt the most considerable work that has ever been written.

AC: But have we not passed here to theology?

BB: No. In terms of metaphysics, Thomas Aquinas synthesized the more than millennial heritage of (neo-)Platonism with the Aristotelianism that had recently "arrived" in Europe. Of course we are still within Christianity here, but at that time all Western thought was quasi-Christian. In other words, the "mysticism" of Platonic philosophy and Christian revelation were well-attuned, and both philosophy and religion were not as yet so opposed, since theology (science or knowledge of God) is part of Aristotle's metaphysics. However, with the introduction of Aristotle into theology by way of Averroes (1126–1198), to the detriment of Avicenna (980–1037), the worm will be in the fruit.

AC: What do you mean?

BB: For Aristotle, the being of the thing to be known is radically different from the being of the knowing subject; this ontological distinction guarantees the objectivity of science. Therefore, knowledge, stripped of its "mystical" dimension, will henceforth be a matter of simple intelligence, and being will remain the affair of religion. Knowledge will no longer be anything but an abstraction and our human existence is left to be dealt with by religion. There is now a division of competence between science and faith, philosophy and religion, nature and supernature, reason and grace (Borella).

AC: This mutual exclusion is asserted by Kant: "I had to suppress knowledge to leave room for faith."

BB: Yes. This is why, even if this balance between science and faith seems solid under the intellectual power of St Thomas Aquinas, it remains fragile (Borella).

AC: How?

BB: The separation does not last long. For example, faith is essentially knowledge, but all knowledge involves faith in what will be found. In these two instances resides a "kernel of gnosis," so much so that a real distinction between science and faith must be refuted (Borella). Moreover, this distinction between knowledge and faith will gradually radicalize. On the one hand, the Lutheran protest will build a faith-without-science and, on the other hand, Cartesianism will erect a science-without-faith, definitively marginalizing theology. And it will be up to Kantian criticism to reject a priori the ontological dimension of knowledge. For him, the real is, by definition, what cannot be known. We glimpse the so-called theologies of the death of God: every concept is an alienating abstraction, even that of God (Vahanian, Hamilton, van Buren…).

AC: I understand from a metaphysical point of view how the Aristotelian reduction of knowledge could produce this sad dynamic, but I did not see St Thomas Aquinas as responsible for such a failure.

BB: He is not. He thought with the available material of his time; and, once again, his synthesis highlights the Neoplatonic tradition with St Augustine and St Dionysius the Areopagite, quoted much more often than Aristotle. Above all, this takes nothing away from the genius of St Thomas Aquinas. And it should be emphasized that, despite his colossal and unequaled work, after an ecstasy experienced towards the end of his life during a religious office, he was able to say that this gigantic work was straw! an illustration, of course, of a humility intrinsic to all true metaphysics as well as to all theology. But this is also a typifying image for any science about the Absolute—as soon as it is led There, it is extinguished.

Still, in the modern era we have a philosophy almost exclusively of the Aristotelian type, which is to say that the object of all knowledge must be of a radically distinct reality. As for theology, it must renounce any union of being and knowing, lest it be accused in such a case of denying revelation and grace and of falling into pantheism (Borella) or ontologism.

AC: But there are plenty of contrary examples, aren't there?

BB: Certainly, but they are on the margins of collective thinking or mainstream, dominant beliefs, which hardly allow them to be heard.

AC: In any case, metaphysics did not stop with St Thomas Aquinas...

BB: That's right.

ST BONAVENTURE. At the time of St Thomas Aquinas there was already an "alternative" to him in the person of St Bonaventure (1217/8–1274), called the Seraphic Doctor. Both died in the same year, and popes Sixtus V (in 1588), and then Leo XIII (in 1879), said they were "two olive trees and two candlesticks." St Bonaventure follows St Augustine and is therefore generally Platonic: for him, metaphysical knowledge is necessarily of a supernatural order (Chenique), whereas St Thomas Aquinas integrates Aristotelian naturalism. Their metaphysics complement each other. As Gilson (1884–1978) puts it, they "neither exclude each other nor coincide."

AC: How is this possible?

BB: This has to do with the connection between creatures and God and access to a knowledge of God. In St Bonaventure we speak of exemplarism: God is the *exemplary* Cause, so that "all creatures are like a shadow, an echo and an image; they are vestiges, symbols... to raise us to the *contuition* ["intuition"] of God." (*Itinerarium* II, 11) They are examples within reach of our minds, "intended to make them pass from the sensible universe, which they see, to the intelligible world, which they do not see, as one passes from the sign to the signified." (Ibid.)

AC: We recognize Plato: the world is "of all necessity the image of something" (*Timaeus*, 29b). It is "in its very substance that the world is endowed with an iconic function" (Borella).

BB: Yes, each physical reality is necessarily the symbol of a metaphysical reality; an ontological link connects them. Conversely, in St Thomas Aquinas, we can speak of analogism: "God lives in an inaccessible dwelling and he would cease to be the Infinite if the finite could symbolize him. Our science of God is constructed using the analogy of proportion/proportionality." (Bernard Landry)

AC: So we see in the Middle Ages this same Plato-Aristotle opposition of Antiquity. Do we find it later?

BB: Yes, we still find it today. This is part of the apparent paradox of the transcendence and immanence of God, that is to say of being both at the heart of and beyond everything—this paradox opens the way to several interpretations. But let's make it the subject of a specific interview.

DESCARTES. (Sigh) I realize that a word must be said about Descartes (1596–1650) and Leibniz (1646–1716), while Meister Eckhart (1260–1328) and so many others must be skipped over, although at least the twentieth-century metaphysicians are left to review. So this will be very brief.

Cartesian metaphysics, found in his *Meditations on First Philosophy*, his *Discourse on Method*, and his *Principles of Philosophy*, starts from doubt in order to attain assured knowledge according to the well-known sequence: I doubt => I think => I am => God is => God guarantees the truth of my knowledge. He is Aristotelian insofar as he marks very little difference between reason and intelligence, but is no longer so when he reduces physics (retaining only the

103

efficient cause) to an integral mechanism (his "animal-machines," for example). He becomes Aristotelian again, however, when physics must be capable of explaining everything. As we can see, his perspective is first of all scientific, and the distinction between an extended thing (*res extensa*)—which Descartes simply calls "corporeal substance"—and a thinking thing (*res cogitans*), which will be much criticized, is more a matter of the method of science than of metaphysics. For Descartes, such a distinction is not really found either in man or in God, so that we can say his so-called dualism "was largely invented after Descartes and projected onto him." (André Charrak, 1969–) In metaphysics, it must be added that his discovery of God does not differ much from that of St Anselm.

AC: I see that you are not using the time-honored formula of "proof of the existence of God" already discussed (see chap. 3).

BB:
LEIBNIZ. I will only say a word about Leibniz. It's sad, because his knowledge was truly encyclopedic, not to mention his qualifications: philosopher, theologian, jurist, historian, mathematician (infinitesimal calculus), physicist, diplomat, adviser to princes and emperors... In metaphysics, we owe him the highlighting of two principles of thought: the principles of sufficient reason and contradiction. And as regards substances (see his *Monadology*), there is the compelling notion of a universe where all things are interrelated (as in quantum physics); and in his *Theodicy* (doctrine of the justice of God), one finds the notions of the "best of all possible worlds" and of "evil for a good" that were present already in St Augustine.

AC: The best of all possible worlds mocked by Voltaire in his *Candide*...

BB: Yes, a considerable publishing success, but at the end of his life Voltaire nevertheless disavowed what he called his own "con-job." But there is one question from Leibniz that struck me. He poses it within the framework of the development of the principle of sufficient reason. There he says: "why is there something rather than nothing?"

AC: A question that eminently contains the answer. Shouldn't this question alone be the subject of an interview?

BB: Certainly. It would also form, in good part, the subject of a whole text entitled "Metaphysics and Cosmology"...

I think we could be briefer with the three twentieth-century metaphysicians I have selected, since we have already spoken of them. We can take them in chronological order.

RENÉ GUÉNON (1886–1951). We have criticized Guénon on the subject of "his" *religio perennis*, his view of the "King of the World," and his partial knowledge of Christianity, but the fact remains that it is appropriate to pay him a strong tribute for his work as a whole. After a century of Kantism and scientific and materialistic triumphalism, he undeniably reopened the way in the West to a sacred intellectuality, to the possibility of supra-rational knowledge— in a word, to a return to a spirituality freed from occultism and so-called esotericism. The West owes a real debt to this most humble man. Millions of pages have been written about him, and I would like to add my own "two cents." First, there are at least two masterpieces: *The Symbolism of the Cross* (1931) and *The Multiple States of the Being* (1932).

With him, Plato is back, intellectual intuition regains its rights. Given the magnitude of this contribution, we understand that, even today, there are many Guénonians, even Guénonists. For my part, I can see a master there, but not the idol he himself would have refused to be. Among a few reservations, I will say that I do not subscribe to the schematic categories of exotericism and esotericism, which are moreover largely absent from Buddhism or Christianity. Or again, after having been much influenced, even marked, by Guénon's critique of the modern world and its "descent" towards a quantitative exclusivity, which he presented in connection with the theory of Hindu cycles or the Greek myth of the World Ages (gold, silver, brass, and iron), I have departed from this interpretation and plan to present the reasons for this in some future book.

AC: A word anyway?

BB: I believe we have seen the Plato-Aristotle alternative persist through the ages and metaphysics, resisting time. Besides, if the iron age, or dark age (*kali yuga*), has been ours for five thousand years and must last another four hundred and twenty-seven thousand years before coming to the end of a cycle that by then will have lasted more than four million years, I do not really see the practical interest of this datum which, although certainly having an esoteric value, seems to me of little interest metaphysically.

AC: Like everything cosmological and temporal compared to the metaphysical and eternity, right?

BB: Exactly!

FRITHJOF SCHUON (1907–1998). The metaphysician Frithjof Schuon wrote many books, and much has been written about him as well—regarding this, I can only be very brief. Like Guénon, he enters metaphysics through *advaita vedanta*, converts to Islam, and critiques the modern world, again within the framework of the theory of cycles of manifestation.

AC: *Advaita vedanta?*

BB: This is the most metaphysical doctrine of the *Vedanta*, taught by the Hindu reformer Sankara in the eighth century. Essentially, this doctrine indicates, depending on the level of reality, that there is only Brahman (Totality, Deity) or, that both *jiva* (the individualized soul) and Ishvara (God as a person) exist, or that all that exists is pure *maya* (illusion). Hence the name *advaita* ("not-two," "non-dual"). This is one of the most fundamental metaphysical paradoxes, allowing us to understand that the creature is both God (only God "really" exists) and not God (it is created within a manifestation). The creature is therefore both one and two, depending on the level of reality considered.

Returning to Schuon, it should be noted that he made a special distinction between reason and intellectual intuition—which in our view makes him a "pure" metaphysician. His understanding of different religions, Native American and Hindu for example, is such that he is able to take his readers to the heart of their sacred mysteries. Some of his books are among the clearest presentations of metaphysics. Let us mention at least his *Logic and Transcendence* (1975) and *Survey of Esoterism and Metaphysics* (1986).

Let's conclude with a word on Perennialism or the Traditionalist School, which brings together at least five metaphysicians, including Guénon and Schuon.

AC: *Sophia Perennis, Religio Perennis,* or *Philosophia Perennis?*

BB: These are indeed the various labels we encounter, with fairly similar meanings, in what can be called the Perennialist School. Essentially, this has to do with—following Nicholas of Cusa (1401–1464) and his *De pace fidei* (1453)—the unity of religions through their metaphysical understanding. It therefore brings together as well five metaphysicians of great value, four of them converts to Islam.

(1) Guénon, the initiator.

(2) Ananda Coomaraswamy (1877–1947), influenced by Guénon, with whom he will have regular communications and, in whose eyes, he will have rehabilitated Buddhism. Convinced of the "Primordial Tradition," he saw in particular *Vedanta* and Platonism as coming from the same origin. Let us cite, among many others, his excellent book *Hinduism and Buddhism* (1943).

(3) Schuon, who knew Guénon directly.

(4) Titus Burckhardt (1908–1984), Schuon's childhood friend (from elementary school). Let us cite, among many others, his book *An Introduction to Sufi Doctrine* (1959).

(5) Leo Schaya (1916–1986), a friend of Schuon, with his *The Universal Meaning of the Kabbalah* (1971) in particular.

For my part, although I do recognize a certain unity of religions, in particular through a metaphysical reading of them, I see little interest in Perennialism as such, and am in any case averse to schools of thought. Moreover, even though these metaphysicians allow us to enter Islam (Sufism), Judaism (Kabbalah), Hinduism, and Buddhism in a quite remarkable way, their contributions to a Christian metaphysics are not very satisfactory. From this point of view, if someone influenced to some extent by Guénon would like to enter into Christianity, it would be necessary to add to these five authors at least Father Stéphane's *Introduction à l'ésotérisme chrétien* ("Introduction to Christian esotericism"), but this is a posthumous publication, centered as it is on the Christian theology, and thus far from a unitive perspective of religious forms.

AC: This interview is coming to an end, and it seems we are left with Jean Borella.

BB: Yes, and a perfect climax to this interview.

JEAN BORELLA (1930–). As he is the one most often quoted (directly or indirectly) authors in all our interviews, I will limit myself to giving a few characteristics of his contributions. As both a Christian and a professional philosopher, with him we can cover the entire history of Western thought, starting with the philosophers of Antiquity, and do so, above all, without excluding either atheist or clerical philosophers, or even scientists when they venture into philosophy—and even when their physics turns out to be fallacious (Galileo). The touchstone is his metaphysical gaze, with its particular gift of shedding light on the history of systems of reasoning. His philosophical critiques are decisive as to the "masters of suspicion."

AC: These masters being Marx, Nietzsche, and Freud (Paul Ricœur, 1913–2005)?

BB: Absolutely, and Borella adds to this list the "physics of suspicion" found in Descartes (the whole world tries to deceive him). Concerning the great denouncers of the universal religious illusion (Feuerbach, Marx, Freud…), he has easily shown how either the denouncers are superhuman (or believe themselves to be such), or the illusion is not universal, since they escape it—thereby making any criticism by the argument of universal illusion obsolete. Detecting contradictions is one his great strengths.

AC: Can you say more?

BB: For example, Kant's claim to limit reason by reason. (*Critique of Pure Reason*, 1781), whereas according to Kant himself, and logically, "what limits must be different from what it limits" (the sea doesn't limit the sea). Or again, Derrida declaring that there are only scattered reasons and "no absolute origin of meaning in general"—so that, were this true, his very declaration would not make sense, and not even for himself. Three key books of Borella should be mentioned here: *The Crisis of Religious Symbolism* (2016), *Histoire et Théorie du Symbol* (2004), and *Penser l'analogie* (2000, 2012).

AC: But not only does his metaphysical gaze focus on philosophical thought, it focuses on theology as well.

BB: Absolutely. And this is where you will find a true metaphysics of the Christian mysteries: *Love and Truth* (2020), *Lumières de la théologie mystique* ["Lights of mystical theology" (2002)], *Un homme une femme au Paradis* ["A Man, a Woman in Paradise" (2008)], *Les sources bibliques de la métaphysique* ["Biblical sources of metaphysics" (2015)], and a few others.

An expert on Guénon, close for some time to Schuon, he was able to develop his own metaphysics by taking a critical step back: *Guénonian Esotericism and Christian Mystery* (2005), republished by Angelico Press in 2018 under the title *Christ the Original Mystery: with special reference to René*

Guénon; *Problems of Gnosis* (2023); *René Guénon et le Guénonisme* ["René Guénon and Guénonism] (2020). Compared to Guénon and Schuon, the issues raised by Borella, and even the rectifications he was led to propose, do not detract from the value of these great metaphysicians. We are here very far from a Kant or a Heidegger repudiating all metaphysics preceding their own existence and contributions.

AC: Wasn't Kant's criticism of a metaphysics reposing in "dogmatic slumber" justified? Especially since he was talking about his own dogmatic slumber?

BB: Actually, Kant limited himself to denying the possibility of metaphysics: "intellectual intuition, in fact, is not ours, and… we cannot even consider the possibility of it." (*Critique of Pure Reason*) To the so-called "dogmatic slumber" of metaphysics, Borella was thus able to counter with Kant's "critical sleep."

AC: You mean when Kant fails to realize that reason cannot limit reason?

BB: Exactly.

PART III

Special Metaphysics

Chapter 8
Metaphysics of Believing

What is believing? and what do we believe when we believe? Considering these questions metaphysically seemed relevant to me, if only to benefit from an outline of what Bruno Bérard plans to do on this subject.

AC: We spoke about your project to write a metaphysics of believing. How did this idea come to you?

BB: What do we believe when we believe? This is of course the question I asked myself.

In the 1960s and 1970s there was a series of books published by Grasset entitled "Ce que je crois" ("What I believe"). Different well-known authors (Jean Guitton, Jacques Ellul, Hervé Bazin, Léopold Sédar Senghor, Bernard Kouchner, etc.) offered their points of view on society, love, death… There we find something *about* metaphysics, especially with Jean Guitton, with his thoughts on just what believing is, or with Jacques Ellul, as a convert to Christianity. There was also the famous *Dieu existe, je l' ai rencontré* ("God exists, I have met him," 1969) by André Frossard (1915–1995), about a revelation during a visit to a chapel in 1935. "I met God as one meets a plane tree. It's a fact, period!" So he wrote some thirty years later.

AC: There is certainly a metaphysics of conversion, and there have been many lightning conversions like the famous one of Israel Zolli (1881–1956), for example. This seems to illustrate adherence to something obvious for

115

some, and not for others. But this doesn't give any indication of the content of belief.

BB: Hence this idea of considering this question metaphysically. "Adherence to something obvious," you said. This first raises the question of believing versus knowing.

To believe or to know?

We often set the believers who believe and the knowers who know in opposition. In this oppositional setting, "believing" pertains to religion and "knowing" to science. But it's not that simple. Can we believe in something we know nothing about? Or again, do we really know something we do not believe? Clearly it is an illusion to think that believing and knowing are mutually exclusive.

AC: But don't we have the cognitive order, which goes from ignorance to knowledge by way of belief?

BB: In fact, it is necessary to add to the cognitive order the volitional order, that is to say the assent that implies the will (Borella). It is even demonstrable that any proof is necessarily a belief.

AC: How so?

BB: There is this perpetual confrontation between these two disjointed domains in the order of rationality: words and things, discourse and facts. "A proposition will be proved if, after having been established by a recognized method, it is the subject of a belief." We have in fact these two disjointed elements: the statement to be proven and the objective apparatus for testing the statement. A first, necessary belief is the recipient's subjective belief in the proof's efficacy; the second, intersubjective belief is a belief in the validity of the procedures of the proof (Fernando Gil, 1937–2006).

AC: Indeed, but these two necessary beliefs are rarely put forward in science.

BB: Yes, because, in science, the technical or practical efficiency often serves as a proof. In any case, we see here that believing and knowing are inseparably combined. When Kant says "I had to suppress knowledge, to find a place for faith," it seems to me that this irreducible combination is missing.

AC: Could you remind me of his reasoning?

BB: He postulates that the metaphysical objects: myself, the world, and God, are unknowable (*Critique of Pure Reason*, 1781), and yet, although they are empirically unknowable (one cannot see, feel, or touch them), it is nevertheless reasonable to *postulate* them as morally necessary *hypotheses*. (*Critique of Practical Reason*, 1788)

AC: It's a balancing act!

BB: Unstable, as soon as one is no longer captivated by rationalist constructions, or, if you will, rationalist reductions.

The next distinction in our approach to believing is between knowing and cognizance.

Knowledge or cognizance?

To go straight to the point, I would say that knowledge is constructed, cognizance is a given.

AC: You need to tell me more.

BB: The world of knowledge is itself paradoxical. On the one hand, what we know is that we know nothing (Socrates/Plato; Montaigne, 1533–1592); but on the other hand, the accumulation of knowledge is obvious in sciences, technologies, craftsmanship. This is because theoretical knowledge always remains plausible hypotheses, while practical knowledge is irrefutable.

Cognizance is something else entirely! It is unable to be generated, it is a pure acknowledgement (Borella): there we have cognizance! That is the intellect, which comes from the outside (Aristotle), as we have said—that is, the understanding that happens, the meaning that reveals itself.

AC: This is what Meister Eckhart says: "The intellect is uncreatable as such"!

BB: Exactly! cognizance is the transcendental condition for any cognitive act. An example is that of light that infuses a crystal. Is it produced by the crystal? And if not, how do we distinguish the intellect from the light it receives? (Borella) We conclude that in its superhuman essence the intellect is uncreated and uncreatable and that "the cognitive content of the intellect exceeds the degree of reality of its manifestation" (Borella), as already quoted.

To believe is therefore to give one's assent to a statement one takes to be true. It can be, for example, a family relationship or that water boils at 100°C; either we will give our confidence to a testimony, or we can verify it empirically by ourselves.

AC: Suffice it to say that for the vast majority of knowledge we trust testimonials, even if very indirect. But what does this have to do with cognizance?

BB: Cognizance is the simple awareness of the power of intelligence as compared to mere reason (Plato), of the supernaturality of the intellect or of intelligible forms (Aristotle), of the ingenerability of meaning or the "semantic principle" (Borella). These are also the examples mentioned during a previous interview: the experience of the thought of the greatest (St Anselm) or God as the source of the thought of God (Descartes). If intelligence is indeed "supernatural by nature" and "metaphysical in essence," if "the intellect already is a divine something" (Borella), the cognizance we are talking about is access—by the nature of this intellect—to what exceeds man.

AC: And can man really know what exceeds him?

What we believe in

BB: We will take the example of Christianity, which is probably the most well-known religion among our readers. Here, the content of believing includes the elements of revelation received by witness through tradition, scripture, and internal "enlightenment" or "theophanic" intellection.

AC: What is involved with this intellection?

BB: Intelligence naturally possesses the power to receive enlightenment; still, it clearly needs to receive it: in Christianity, this is the initiation of baptism, confirmation, and the Eucharist. It is the actualization, through sacramental initiation into divine filiation, of the power of the intellect to be naturally ordered to the supernatural (Borella).

If theology is by definition the science of God, knowledge of God is lived theology.

AC: Isn't that mystical, then?

BB: We're getting there. St Dionysius the Areopagite distinguishes four successive paths (or modes) of theology, and it is crucial that we understand these as regards the content of believing we are talking about. I will follow here what Jean Borella has written on the subject.

(1) With SYMBOLIC THEOLOGY the intelligence reads the symbols (rock, cross, light, etc.), which are made explicit to it. We then receive "in these forms a teaching that escapes any form" (René Roques, 1927–2019); we grasp "in the figure of these realities, the realities without figure" (Borella).

AC: Can you say a word about symbols, especially given that they form the basis for one of Jean Borella's major works?

BB: In short, the symbol *ontologically* connects something visible to something invisible in the form of a "dissimilar similarity" (René Roques, 1917–). *Similarity* is a static link, it is the analogical nature of the symbol. As for *dissimilarity*, it causes the image that is to be renounced to rise dynamically towards the model: this is the anagogic virtue of the symbol (Borella).

(2) With AFFIRMATIVE THEOLOGY we enter the field of the conceptually intelligible, of discursive reason and therefore of language. We start from God as revealed in scripture and follow the descending order of the procession of divine immanence according to the degrees of Creation: One or Good, Being, Life, Intelligence… until, through distancing, its possibilities are exhausted.

(3) NEGATIVE THEOLOGY, then, will deny any symbol and any concept asserted previously, since God is still beyond all that. The concept is no longer a simple mental object, but becomes a *metaphysical operator*: once the mental object is denied, theological intelligence can become aware of the transcen-

dent reality that it designates. The model is transcendent to its reflection in thought.

AC: We find here again the principle of Plato's analogical line (*cf.* Appendix I), as well as this idea of the extinction of metaphysics once it has accomplished its function.

BB: Absolutely. We can say that to symbolic theology corresponds vision, to affirmative (rational) theology corresponds discourse, and to negative (intellectual) theology corresponds intuition. Thus, negative theology makes it possible to "realize the unity of seeing (symbol) and conceiving (concept); the symbol: vision without intellection, and the concept: intellection without vision." (Borella)

(4) We then access an intellective vision that pertains to MYSTICAL THEOLOGY.

AC: So what is the difference between negative theology and mystical theology?

BB: It is simply the difference between the path and the end of the path. In mystical theology "intelligence has closed its eyes," as St Dionysius the Areopagite has said, in the presence of what in any case "is above the eyes" (Malebranche, 1638–1715).

AC: To believe, then, is to no longer know anything?

What is it to believe?

BB: In terms of rational or conceptual knowledge, absolutely; but if we are speaking about cognizance, not quite. Allowing intellectual intuition to operate leads to this already mentioned knowledge by participation. We might just as well speak of contemplation or gnosis.

AC: Gnosis?

BB: There are many Greek terms with reference to knowledge (*episteme, dianoesis, gnomè, logos, mathesis, noesis, phronesis*, etc.), but *gnosis* has taken on a very specific meaning. In Plato, it means *pure* cognizance; in the Old Testament, it is *absolute* cognizance, that of God— it even designates not only an *act*, but also a *state* (Rudolf Bultmann, 1884–1976). In the New Testament, we find it especially in St Paul. With the incarnation of the divine *Word*, of the *Logos*, Christianity is a gnostic religion *par excellence*; it is even gnosis itself in all its purity (Borella). But two things must be clarified with regard to this gnosis and the belief about which we are speaking:

(1) As a state, only God can confer gnosis on the "pneumatized intellect." (Borella)

AC: Can you elaborate on "pneumatized intellect"?

BB: We can also say "spiritualized intellect"; "pneuma" is the "breath" in Greek and therefore the spirit. In the Old Testament it was used to translate the Hebrew *ruach* (spirit). It is, once again, that Light which enlightens the intellect, and without which only an ineffectual mental power remains.

(2) On the side of the one who believes, to believe is to renounce knowledge, or to recognize one's "ontological ignorance" (Borella). We then speak of *epignosis* or supra-knowledge (St Paul), of "gnosis by nescience" (Borella), or of "learned ignorance." (Nicholas of Cusa, 1401–1464)

AC: These are oxymorons!

BB: Yes, this is the means proposed to go further than the simple philosophical observation that what we know is that we know nothing. The metaphysical or spiritual awareness, from which everyone can benefit, is this fully conscious renunciation. We will also find it in Montaigne, Descartes, Pascal... But this renunciation is not enough, there is still someone who renounces.

AC: So how far should we go?

BB: To the end! And this end is the only Principle, it is the Absolute in regard to which the individual is strictly null, to put it like Guénon. Just as abruptly, it is what we read in the Old Testament: "there is nothing outside Him" (Isaiah), or in Shankara: "nothing else exists but the Self," or again with Ibn 'Arabi: "outside the Principle, there is absolutely nothing that exists." From this point of view, we can say that "to become Nothing is to become God" (Angelus Silesius).

AC: My understanding is that if we take being in the strong sense there is nothing other than God, or the Absolute, the Infinite, the Principle, etc., but that there is indeed this "sallying forth out of nothing" resulting in the beings that we are, right?

BB: Yes, in the belief we are talking about, there is someone who believes, but only at the start. Because the bottom line of believing is to annihilate oneself and forget that one has done it; it is *to lose consciousness*. At the end of it all, what remains is pure belief. In Christian language, we speak of a sacrifice, like that of the divine Logos, dead and risen.

AC: How can anyone go any further?

BB: I believe that is the end of the end of believing. We could perhaps append some striking texts by St Dionysius the Areopagite, Meister Eckhart, St Thomas Aquinas...

AC: Good idea (see Appendix III)!

Chapter 9

Metaphysics of Sex

While metaphysics is primarily concerned with the Absolute, it might surprise you to see it dealing with a seemingly prosaic subject like sex. I take advantage of an interview to clarify what a metaphysics of sex is.

AC: Where did this subject of a metaphysics of sex come from? Is it about sexuations or the sexual act? And what about gender issues?

Context of a metaphysics of sex

BB: That's a lot of questions at once. Let's start with the context; it is triple. First there is the famous book by Julius Evola, which in 1958 posed the subject in its title. As he specifies in the introduction, however, he renounces metaphysics as such in favor of a study of the transphysiological and transpsychological aspects of sex. The title of his book is therefore confusing.

AC: There is also the fact that, since this book, much time has elapsed, with, in particular, gender studies, changes in the status of homosexuals, scientific discoveries in matters of sexuation and sexuality, academic work on sexual esotericism, even a certain change in the positions of the Catholic Church: I am thinking of Benedict XVI's *Theology of the Body* or certain positions of Pope Francis…

BB: Absolutely. Also, there is the fact that to my knowledge this subject has not been treated, except in a piecemeal way here or there. We have already mentioned all these celibate philosophers, who were able to speak about love, like Plato, or exceptionally of sex, but make it a contractual exchange of possession of the body of the other within the framework of a marriage (Kant), or reduce it to a supposed reproductive instinct (Schopenhauer). Finally, there were my own questions about it, especially related to the fact that, for some, there is never any sexual act, while for others, this is a frequent activity, even up to being expressed sordidly. Why then a systematic sexuation and an optional sexuality that can even vary *ad infinitum*?

AC: Could you say more?

BB: An Indian professor of forensic medicine (Anil Aggrawal, 1956–) listed 547 paraphilias (new name for what used to be called sexual perversions).

AC: Impressive! Sex has resources! But apart from philosophy are we not already aware of many books on sex, especially related to religions?

BB: Certainly, but while I wanted to make it a "universal" work, these studies are linked to particular religions: there is *Eros juif* ("Jewish Eros," David Biale), *Kabbalah and Eros* (Moshe Idel), *The Sacrament of Love* (Paul Evdokimov), *Christianity and Eros* (Philip Sherrard), *La mystique du couple* ("The Mysticism of the Couple," Alphonse and Rachel Goettmann) or *Eros sauvé* ("Eros Saved," Jean Bastaire), *Alchemy of Love: Sexuality and the Spiritual Life* (M.S. de Azevedo, Schuon, Burckhardt, et al). All of these books are remarkable and I took as many elements from them as possible.

AC: What method did you follow for this investigation?

Sexuations, genders, sexuality, an inventory

BB: I started by drawing up an inventory of sexuations, genders, sexualities, and their management in societies.

AC: Could you summarize?

BB: Concerning the sexuations, we distinguish a multitude of different sexes, no longer allowing the congealing of human beings into two disjointed *categories*, male and female; however, in terms of *types*, male and female remain unavoidable. Regarding gender, it seems that their proliferation in modern societies compensates for the absence of a third sex, a category common to all traditional societies. The claimed modern genders curiously do not involve eliminating male-female sexism but seem rather to involve having society recognize all possible cases. Moreover, these cases mix the types of sexuation (intersex, trans), the genders (queer, two-spirit), the types of sexuality (lesbian, sado-masochist)... And interesting questions arise around borderline cases: for instance, a man who is a woman on the inside and has a sexual relationship with a woman—is this a homosexual or heterosexual relationship?

AC: Good question! And what about love?

Where does love stand in all of this?

BB: This is the second part of the study: the reciprocal exclusion of love and sex, or else their harmonious combination. My conclusion is that their rare reciprocal exclusion is pathological (Otto Weininger, 1880–1903); otherwise, sex and love are both separable and reunitable.

AC: And is there no better or ideal situation?

BB: Of course, on the one hand we find a high percentage of men ready to make love with a robot, but sociological studies confirm that the preferable and most preferred situation is when the sexual act takes place within a love relationship. Very specifically, we see that the love relationship transcends the sexual relationship. Sexual techniques do not appear to be essential.

AC: What are these sexual techniques?

Sexual techniques

BB: I found three of those, typical from the cultural areas where they appeared.

There is tantra in India, which can include sacred and ritualized sexual acts; sex is then a means of meeting the divine, the marriage of Shiva and Shakti.

Tao, or sexual kung fu, in China, seemed to me to be essentially medicine, in the sense of maintaining good health and long life.

Karezza, in the West, which relates to psychological comfort, in particular by offering a means of natural contraception (unreliable) that does not deprive the partners of sexual pleasure.

AC: Mysticism, good health, and psychological comfort sum up the cultural characteristics of these three regions; are there no common points?

BB: There is one, yet technical; it is, for the man, the retention of ejaculation. This is an interesting point, in that it makes it possible to distinguish three functions of the sexual organs: urination, pleasure, and reproduction. The child is asked to control urination to forestall enuresis, the adult man will be asked to control ejaculation to forestall "ejacularesis." The bottom line is that it is controllable and distinct from a male's orgasm. If there is a species pole with

reproduction, there is indeed an individual pole with pleasure, which neurobiology amply confirms.

AC: And where are we metaphysically at this stage?

Metaphysics of sex and the sexes

BB: This is the third part of this study, which can now
begin. Up to this point, we only have two of the three
aspects of the traditional tripartition of the human being:
body, soul, spirit, or, in more modern language: body,
psyche, spirit. What this part will now show is that sexual
love is the only human act that actively brings into play the
whole of the human being, his bodily, psychic, and spiritual
dimensions.

AC: Can you illustrate?

BB: Of course, in part, I present what a metaphysics of sex
obviously is not, with sexual magic, sexual esotericisms
(Böhme, Swedenborg) and, very prosaically, sexual meta-
phors compared to the symbols that can be developed (the
world axis, the cave). Complementarily, a spirituality of the
union of sexual love presents the virtues and the mysticism
of such a union.

AC: So much for the sexual act, but what about the origin
of the two sexes?

BB: The two standard sexes necessarily have their source in
the Principle. Ibn ʿArabi (thirteenth century) makes sexual
union the general model of causality (cosmogony, anthro-
pology). I benefited here from an excellent study by Mensia
Arfa Mokdad, which I used copiously. Jean Borella, in his
meditations on Genesis (2008), shows how the doubling
(qualitative feminine-masculine, and not just the quantitative one plus one) actualizes the existence of Adam and Eve

(they only exist one by the other). If the natural function of the human being is to be the image of God within creation, this iconic function requires the duality of the sexes. It is integral to the relationship between man and woman ("there is no masculine except for the feminine and vice versa"), which is the image of God in the order of creation—image, that is to say, in relation to its Model. Thus, the conjugal relationship is the image of the relationship of the human being to his Creator: "Here is the metaphysical foundation of the duality of the sexes!" (Borella)

AC: But "why this rather than that?" Leibniz would ask, since women and men individually have the theomorphic function (of the image of God).

BB: They do not exercise it in the same way. In every image: there is "an 'essential' or 'formal' aspect (in the sense of Aristotle) and an 'existential' or 'material' (receptacular) aspect." It is not a matter of a *bipartition,* but of a functional *polarization:* "each sex carries within itself the entirety of the divine image . . . each, in its vertical relationship, which unites within it human nature to its Creator, is neither masculine nor feminine." (Borella)

AC: Hence such declarations as: "in the resurrection, they neither marry nor are given in marriage" (Matt. 22:30) or "there is neither male nor female" (Gal. 3:28)?

BB: Yes, in the earthly order, the "entities" discover that they exist thanks to the relations of all orders; in the celestial order, the primacy is in the relation; Being is primarily relational.

AC: I am very much looking forward to reading this upcoming book. Indeed, no work, to my knowledge, has offered such a panorama covering sexuation, gender, and

sexuality in the light of religions, philosophies, and techniques, with a metaphysical interpretation of the sexes and
the sexual act.

Chapter 10
Metaphysics and Matter

If God is so to speak at one end of metaphysics, do we not see matter at the other end? How then does metaphysics consider matter? This is what I wanted to clarify during this interview.

AC: Metaphysics has been able to lead us, with Meister Eckhart, even beyond God; would matter be at the other end? What is matter in metaphysics?

BB: I think it would be interesting to review the distinct understandings that different approaches have about matter.

Matter—scientific understanding

If I may summarize very succinctly: known matter is 99.99% vacuum and, according to the current standard model of particle physics, represents only 5% of the universe. Moreover, the model does not integrate gravity at the quantum level, and the dark matter hypothesis would have to be confirmed to verify the Big Bang model.

AC: It is impressive that quantum physics might one day explain both the world of particles and that of the universe, so as to confirm the current cosmological model of the Big Bang.

BB: As always with science, quantum mechanics has enabled concrete techniques like lasers and light-emitting diodes, for example, but we are very far from a complete description of the universe. If, as Wolfgang Smith shows, there is a "vertical causality," current physics cannot come to any satisfying conclusion.

AC: Can you summarize his approach?

BB: In short, what I understand is that he applies to the principle of quantum superposition—the bodily object and its "associated physical object"—the Aristotelian concepts of *potency and act*, as well as the notion of *substantial form*, while quantum physics reduces the corporeal object to pure quantities, eclipsing all qualities present in the world. In cosmology, he shows that, according to the theory of relativity itself, heliocentrism and geocentrism both have scientific value, in particular because observations made from the Earth are *de facto* geocentric. And, quite recently, he has proposed a demonstration of an "ontologization" of the principle of Rolf Landauer (1927–1999),[1] but this is not the place to explain it.

AC: I understand, but is it likely to redirect physics?

BB: For the time being, I'm not sure. There are three reasons for this. First, since Aristotle, qualities seem forever excluded from a science defined by mathematical abstraction and proceeding exclusively by quantification. Secondly, the Aristotelian teleological cause has become anti-scientific. Thirdly, the *models* of physics are necessarily long-lived, and it takes a lot of contradictory observations for them to be modified.

---

[1] Working for IBM, this physicist showed that "*Information is physical*" because when information is lost or erased in some IT system, it becomes entropy while a corresponding quantity of energy is dissipated as heat. This principle applies to reversible computing, as well as quantum information and computing.

AC: Do you have an example?

BB: There is the assumption of a ubiquitous, homogeneous, and isotropic universe, which is useful for solving the equations of general relativity. It *seemed* to be supported by the almost perfect isotropy of the "cosmic microwave background" (or microwave radiation filling all space) and was supported by the model of "cosmic inflation" (which makes possible the transition from a disordered initial state to a homogeneous and isotropic state). However, the colossal cluster of quasars (the Huge-LQG: Huge Large Quasar Group), recently discovered (2013), calls into question the level of homogeneity defined by this cosmological model.

AC: So we are not ready to shift to some new standard cosmological model.

BB: I do not believe so. But we should move on now to how matter is understood philosophically.

Materia—philosophical understanding

Philosophically, matter is the substance of the world before it receives a determined form. According to Plato, it is pure receptivity, indeterminacy, and passivity. Next, Aristotle will further define this passivity with the notions of potency and act: matter is a being in potentiality; form is a being in act. At one extreme we have God as pure act (*actus purus*), at the other extreme we have *materia prima*, pure undifferentiated potentiality. Between the two, all beings are a combination of actuality and potentiality according to the different determinations that are either actualized or in potency.

AC: Or we can say that beings combine being and non-being, as we saw in Plato.

BB: Yes. In St Thomas Aquinas, it is interesting to see that prime matter (*materia prima*) is the first principle of individuation of bodily substances, followed by a natural bodily quantity (*materia signata quantitate*) which gives matter its three-dimensionality—something required by any substantial form of any corporeality.

AC: I do not understand everything!

BB: Me neither (laughs). There are tens of thousands of pages to read—and to understand!—on this simple subject of individuation. The main take-away is that, in philosophy, we distinguish between the *materia*, the medium, and the form; and above all, that prime matter is undifferentiated and unintelligible. Moreover, there is also an interesting cosmic substance to consider in different traditions.

Cosmic substance—a traditional understanding

In the languages of India, this cosmic substance comes close to Sarasvati, Lakshmi, and Parvati, the consorts of Brahma, Vishnu, and Shiva. In Judaism, there is *Malkuth*, the tenth sefirot, called "daughter" or "inferior Mother" (while *Binah* is "superior Mother"), because she is the passive and direct cause of cosmic "construction." *Malkuth* comprises the immanent *Shekhinah-Metatron-Avir* Tri-Unity in which *Metatron* is the cosmic Act and Measure by which the *Shekhinah* determines the forms of all created things and *Avir*, the substantial principle, is the universal and undifferentiated ether which is the elusive "circumference" of the world. *Metatron* is the active and ordering aspect of divine immanence, *Avir* is its envelope, the substantial cause of creation (Leo Schaya). In Islam, al-Hayula (cosmic substance) is clearly distinguished from al-Haba (principial substance or *materia prima*), which can be contrasted with al-'Aql al-awwal (the first intellect).

AC: And in Christianity?

Creation ex nihilo—the Christian understanding

BB: In Christianity, we have the doctrine of *creatio ex nihilo* and the metaphysical notion of "cosmic charity" (Borella). The precise formula is *productio rei ex nihilo sui et subjecti*. All production is *ex nihilo sui*, that is to say that the form produced did not exist before; but also *ex nihilo subjecti*, which means that there did not exist any pre-existing matter from which and in which the form would have been produced by God. Creation *ex nihilo* therefore means that God is the sole cause, both formal and substantial (Chenique). But to proceed further, we must consider this complete formula: *Creatio ex nihilo a Deo per Verbum in Spiritu Sancto*:

Ex nihilo, as we have just seen;

a deo means that creation is "by God"; it is neither *ex deo* (emanation, hence a pantheism by absence of radical transcendence) nor *in deo* (in God, therefore unmanifest);

per Verbum means that the Father creates *through* the Word (He contains the exemplary causes of all things): "through him everything was made" (Col. 1:16; John 1:3);

if the Father proceeds through the Son to create the world, where does He create it? *In* the Holy Spirit: *in Spiritu Sancto!*

"God casts His Divine Charity before Himself and by this He creates the exteriority wherein He will be able to project

135

creatures. But because this exteriority is charity, it is love of God and leads everything back to Him, being nothing but the mode according to which God comes toward Himself out of His own Beyond." (Borella)

AC: Can we therefore say that, in Christianity, we bathe in the Holy Spirit?

BB: I do think so myself. However, it is the immanence of God that is in question, i.e., space as *sensorium Dei* (Newton)—the place in which God perceives everything by his immediate presence. The *materia prima* is already the created substrate of manifestation.

AC: What conclusion have you drawn from this overview of the various understandings of matter?

Metaphysical conclusions

BB: I find all scientific efforts admirable, especially in the search for a theory of everything, but I think that, looking at stars or particles, the bottom line is forever scientifically unknowable.

> COSMOLOGY. Within "a universe that begins to look more like a great thought than a great machine" (James Jeans, 1877–1946), we find the teaching of Plato: any cosmology can only be "a probable myth." Moreover, the search for limits is impossible, since, metaphysically, neither the beginning nor the end of space is part of it and, similarly, neither the beginning nor the end of time is part of it, by definition. In terms of space and time, the model comes up against Planck's wall.

> MATTER. The same goes for matter. Great physicists have given up: "The metaphysical real world is

therefore not the starting point of scientific research, but its inaccessible goal" (Max Planck, 1858–1947), and even proposed a metaphysical solution: "there is no matter in itself. [...] we must admit [...] a conscious and intelligent Spirit. This Spirit is the principle of all matter." (Max Planck)

"In quantum physics, a dog is a wave function and is inseparable from the wave function of the rest of the Universe, since the quantum conception implies a globality, according to which there is only one wave function, that of the Universe . . . physics does not need to assume that this reality exists or does not exist." (Marc Lachièze-Rey, 1950–)

AC: Is it therefore no longer the real that is sought by science?

BB: That's what it seems, yes. We had the ancestral ontology of substance, then the ontology, still material, of matter-energy (Einstein); it is now an "ontology of the absence of substrate," which emerges with field theory, quantum mechanics, information theory, and the theory of dynamical systems, which are complicit in putting dematerialized concepts such as process or information at the forefront of our vision of the world. "It is the world of the signal that is gaining traction. An objectless universe, where only the signs matter." (Simon Diner)

AC: This is where metaphysics regains all its rights.

BB: Rights that it has, I believe, never lost, despite having been supposed impossible (Kant), insane (Carnap), deconstructable (Derrida) or even led astray into ontotheology (Heidegger). Thus, a recent physicist recommended con-

137

sidering, in physics, a metaphysics of a Platonic (cave symbol) or Aristotelian (potency and act) type. He has even declared:

> In view of contemporary physics, I say that if we desperately need an explanation, we have to seek it in what is higher than ourselves, and that is therefore mysterious to us. It is the Real, Being itself, the Divine. It is from this side that we can hope to discern its meaning. (Bernard d'Espagnat)

The physicist Bernard d'Espagnat (1921–2015) has ventured to suggest researching upstream of the relativity of time, such as "eternity" and "continuous creation" (notions to be adapted of course to physics). Also, he suggests relating his "extended causality" to the Aristotelian final cause ("as the real is first in relation to time, the causality that it exercises cannot be subjected to a strict condition of anteriority"). He proposes relating his own concept of "veiled reality" to Aristotle's potency and act. Following Heisenberg (1901–1976) and reinforced by the recent theory of decoherence, he proposes relating *materia prima* to the "wave function of the Universe." He also proposes, rightly it seems to me, to relate the "veiled reality" of the myth of Plato's cave to a parallel between the Platonic Good and the "real." Far from any idealism, this is Plato's "realism of essences." And this is what the physicist Bryce DeWitt (1923–2004) would also suggest:

> To take quantum mechanics at face value is to consider this theory as the true reality, that is, as belonging to the Platonic domain of ideal essences.

Chapter 11
Metaphysics and the *Post-Mortem* State

While its easy to see that, as far as God is concerned, only his existence—and thus the origin of being and beings—is evident, the question that arises is that of the future of these beings, especially their post-mortem fate. What is the future of being and of all those beings who are dying and disappearing every moment in the world? Does metaphysics have anything to say on this subject?

AC: We understand that there is a Principle at the origin of being and of beings, and that this "source" is transcendent to them and contains, to infinity, all the perfections whose reflections we see around us (life, personality, love, beauty, etc.). So, if a "what's before?" gets a relatively obvious answer, what does metaphysics answer to "what's next?"

BB: To my knowledge, metaphysics as such, that is to say as a science, has no answer to this question. It can speak about the resorption of manifestation in the principle and, if we agree that it is "strictly nil with respect to the Infinite" (Guénon), are we not then tempted to conclude that the end of the journey obliterates the journey in its entirety?

AC: What you are saying is that manifestation is null—and void—before, during, and after its end, which would mean that it never existed!

From the origin of being

BB: This is indeed what one might be led to think. But we prefer the view that the Good (and the Beautiful and the True) is part of the Principle, beyond being, beyond the essence (*épékeïna tès ousias*) as Plato specifies (*Republic*, VI, 509b), and that it is "diffusive of itself" (*Bonum diffusivum sui*, St Thomas Aquinas), which is to say that it is the Good that gives being to things.

AC: This is the formula "God is Love" (1 John 4:8) in Christianity. For that matter, even though there might be some mechanism to distribute being, it would still be necessary to figure out the designer and builder of this "machine."

Beyond Being

BB: And so we come to the "after": if the origin is the Good, the end is necessarily also the Good.

AC: Hence the various paradises of religions...

BB: Absolutely, but if we stick to metaphysics, then we have to abandon metaphysics as a science for metaphysics as a path. If we experience being as a gift, and are therefore experiencing the Giver, this experience is necessarily of a "mystical" order.

AC: You mean that here we are going beyond the order of concepts...

BB: Yes. In other words, the Good of Plato (or the Godhead of Meister Eckhart or the modern Beyond-Being of Schuon) is beyond all duality and beyond unity as well as multiplicity; it is the "more than luminous Darkness." (St Dionysius the Areopagite)

AC: Deep "Darkness," but by excess of brilliance!

BB: Absolutely! Above all, "there" (so to speak) are no more oppositions; we are beyond opposites. The principle of non-contradiction, essential to the world of concepts, no longer applies. It is absolute Non-Contradiction, the "coincidence of opposites." (St Bonaventure, then Nicholas of Cusa)

AC: What you are saying then is that there is no opposition between the multiplicity of beings and the unique Being.

BB: Exactly. There is no massive identification or resorption in the Principle: identity and alterity are necessarily combined (Borella). Above all, we will have gained access to a metaphysics of relationship. As already mentioned, what matters is no longer the insoluble paradox of the single Being and multiple beings, but the relationships that exist within Being. Being is first of all relational, as we have already said.

AC: Can you elaborate a bit?

BB: There exists in Christianity an incomparable doctrine that throws light on this question. We could always transpose it into metaphysics, but what's the point! This doctrine is of course linked to the Incarnation; not the incarnation of God as such, but that of God-the-Son, the *Logos* or the divine Word. From there, we have a key to resolve the apparent paradox of beings and Being—for the origin of the world, for earthly life, and for the prospect of the afterlife.

AC: I'm all ears!

BB: Let us first recall that this vertical axis of the world is Christ (in the Incarnation), the Word (at the origin of the worlds), and the Son (in the Trinity, beyond all worlds).

The origin of the worlds is in the Word, the place of all possibilities and intelligible forms (St Augustine). God does everything *by* the Word or *through* Him.

AC: It is in the text: "his Son, whom he appointed *heir of all things*, and *through whom* also he made the worlds." (Heb. 1:2)

BB: Yes, or "For by him were all things created, that are in heaven, and that are in earth, visible and invisible... all things were created by him and for him." (Col 1:16) And there are still many other texts that say the same thing. In summary, the Word, or the *Logos*, to give it its metaphysical meaning, is much more than a simple link, it even resolves the transcendence-immanence paradox in its own way through the distinction between *essence* and *power*:

> Present in all creation, the Word remains exterior to everything according to its essence, but He is in everything by His power, ordering all things and unfolding His providence everywhere towards all things, quickening each being and all beings at the same time. (St Athanasius, *On the Incarnation of the Word*, §17)

The Christological hologram

Being all in all, the Word is the divine Hologram through-out all Creation.

AC: Hologram? The one found in Jules Verne's *Carpathian Castle* (1892), and that later gave rise to the laser technique?

BB: That same one! A hologram is only a three-dimensional image, but with the particularity that the whole (*holos*) is inscribed (*graphein*) in each part. The analogy becomes obvious: it is "the fullness of Him who fills all in all" (Eph. 1:23), the Word, the *Logos*.

AC: And then after death?

BB: Before getting there, there still is the earthly human existence to consider. The vertical Son-Word-Christ is relation *par excellence*: as Son, he is the (subsisting) relationship of God to God, and as Word he is the (ontological) relationship between the created and the Uncreated; moreover, what interests us here is that, as Christ, he is the relationship of proximity. He is *the preeminent Neighbor*, the metaphysical foundation of the relation of proximity, integral to the neighbor (Borella).

AC: It is *by* or *through* Him, then, that people mutually enter into close relationships. Hence the love of neighbor!

BB: And without forgetting the love of enemies! We cannot divide the neighbor into segments, decide who is and who is not our neighbor; they are all part of Christ, they are all Christ, the only Neighbor. Here we have the famous: "who receives you receives me" (Matt. 10:40) or "all that you have done to one of the least of my brothers, you have done it to me." (Matt. 25:40)

This is His "hologrammity" in the world!

AC: I see taking shape here just how life-after-death will be presented.

BB: Yes indeed! But I would like to point out several things: First of all, as you called to mind, there is not, metaphysically, such a great difference between the Platonic Good and the God-Love of Christianity (or, for that matter, the Compassionate and Merciful God of Islam, etc.). Therefore, the Christ of the Christians personifies—from earth to heaven—the destination of the relationship of love. The end of the act of love is not others as such, but others as neighbor; and the only neighbor is Christ. In other words, "the neighbor is the matter of proximity, Christ [Word-Son] is its eternal Form." (Borella) Moreover, if Christ is in every human being—his hologrammity—this means that each of us is Christ for others.

AC: It is a paradox: we are all the Christ of all the others, but of course none of us is *the* Christ. The hologram is both the image of the essence that is beyond, and the image of the power that is in everyone.

BB: Yes, Christ remains the Totally Other; and God is the Otherness *par excellence*. Here we have a "mystical" conversion of the horizontal other to the vertical Other. These are the first two Commandments, of which the second is said to be like unto the first one.

AC: "Thou shalt love the Lord thy God" and "Thou shalt love thy neighbor as thyself." (Matt. 22:37, 39)

BB: We can now talk about the afterlife.

The afterlife

A glimpse into the afterlife is granted us and summed up in the *promise* of Christ: "That they all may be one; as thou, Father, art in me, and I in thee, that they also may be one in us." (John 17:21) It is always this image of the hologram that can help us think about it.

AC: This means that there is a kind of "obligatory" solidarity between all human beings, right?

BB: Absolutely, this solidarity comes from the unique source that is the *Logos*, in which all beings are formed.

Whether we call him Christ or not, he is the one source of all. Creation in this sense overtops and overflows the religions. This solidarity comes just as much from the unique destination of beings. To renounce it as long as there remains a being to be "saved" is, moreover, a way at least common to Buddhism and Christianity: St Thérèse of Lisieux is a Christian boddhisatva (Chenique).

AC: How would you conclude this interview?

BB: We could let Meister Eckhart do it: "all creatures gather in my intellect, so that, in me, they become intelligible. I alone prepare them to return to God"—however, without forgetting the metaphysical operator that is Love, both in the creation of beings and their terminal in-gathered solidarity.

AC: It is what we said at the beginning: the Good—beyond being—is the origin and the end.

Chapter 12

Conclusion:
What is Metaphysics?

Last in this series of twelve interviews, it seemed to me that it would be useful to offer readers a sort of synthesis of what metaphysics is according to Bruno Bérard.

AC: To conclude our interviews, could you answer this question: What is metaphysics?

BB: So far, to illustrate metaphysics, we have started with examples: matter, sex, belief, or comparisons with science, religion, esotericism, mysticism. I suggest reversing the approach: starting from what metaphysics is (in my opinion), then seeing how it applies, step by step, to the whole world, to life, to death.

AC: Is death to end on a happy note? (laughs)

BB: Well yes, I will try to show it cheerfully.

Metaphysics as epiphany of the spirit

Metaphysics is an epiphany of the Spirit—a formula borrowed from Jean Borella—that is to say, a manifestation of the Spirit in the human being. Indeed, this may even seem surprising after the affirmation of the death of God and the reduction of man to a simple body.

AC: We talked about this rather fictitious death of God. But what do you mean by the reduction of the human being to a simple body?

BB: Very simply, at all times and in all places our human condition was deemed tripartite: body, psyche, and spirit. Some have even thought, in the wake of St Augustine, that "the Spirit is that of the Father and of the Son and *ours*"— God's immanence. After Descartes and especially Kant, the human being was reduced to the duality of body and psyche. Finally, with evolutionism, psychoanalysis, and neuro-psychologism, the human being is apparently nothing more than a body from which emanates thoughts according to more or less identified determinisms.

AC: And on this point...?

BB: This last stage has even been philosophically "scored" with the affirmation of a decentered and dispersed reason in individuals (Derrida).

AC: Can you explain more?

BB: We have seen intelligence or intellect fathom and complete reason: on the one hand, as the faculty of understanding what reason has calculated; and on the other, as the faculty of intuition and access to reality, that is, a human agency open to a light that goes beyond it, a "sense of the supernatural" (Borella), one might say.

AC: I see.

BB: It was then that Descartes, although a true metaphysician, nevertheless tended to collapse the two faculties, reason and intelligence, into one. What remained was the body and the psyche: this is that Cartesian dualism attributed to Descartes *a posteriori*. Kant then went so far as to invert them, placing reason at the peak of the human faculties, since intellectual intuition had no meaning for him; and below reason was a practical intelligence that would

147

become the object of psychology and IQ testing.

AC: Great, a measure of intelligence, so we will finally know what it is! Just kidding (laughs)!

BB: But you're not far from the actual story. To the question: "What is intelligence?" the inventors of the IQ test (Alfred Binet, 1857–1911 and Théodore Simon, 1873–1961) replied (so it is said): "but that is precisely what our test measures!" In their defense, we recognize the value of their pragmatic approach for educational use. In any case, after the Kantian inversion, it became logical to describe intelligence as agility of mind or capacity for mental arithmetic, which notwithstanding does relate to reason. (In this respect, the term "artificial intelligence" is quite amiss; the better choice would have been "artificial *reason*," the mental or calculating power man has conferred on himself thanks to computers.)

AC: And the final phase? Or should we say *terminal* phase?

BB: Since there was only one reason surmounting a body, it remained to be deconstructed, and Derrida took charge of this. For him, reason is no longer a common good, meaning it is completely indeterminate. And so, from a reasonable animal, we come in the end to the body only, a living corpse, a zombie.

AC: But not everyone is involved in these narratives, whether they are about the death of God or this death of man, right?

BB: In fact, these thinkers will have only been mirroring the *episteme* of their time.

AC: *Episteme?*

BB: In Foucault's sense (1926–1984)—that is, that which is on people's minds at a given time. Thus, Kant's thought is only the reflection of the Enlightenment on its dark side, that is to say the little individual light, with all the obscurantism we recognize in it today. The more recent *episteme*, the one expressed by Derrida, is imbued, in addition to the ideology of psychoanalysis and the necessarily materialist methodologies of the neurosciences, with the now out of fashion "chance" of a Jacques Monod (1910–1976), which had led him to think that "man knows at last that he is alone in the universe's unfeeling immensity, out of which he emerged only by chance. His destiny is nowhere spelled out, nor is his duty." (*Chance and Necessity*, trans. A. Wainhouse [New York: Alfred A. Knopf, 1971], 180)

AC: So, back to the beginning, far from these "trends," metaphysics is to experience again and again the intelligence or the intellect as a receiver of light or meaning, and to recognize that they are transcendent to it.

BB: This is for me the essential point of metaphysics, its possibility and its point of departure. From there, metaphysics becomes a universal and "final arbiter."

AC: How?

Metaphysics as a universal and final arbiter

BB: Its anchoring in the recognition of something transcendent gives it an overarching point of view. This transcendent acts as an absolute in relation to the relativity of the world. From there, all the material and formal objects of the sciences, of all possible knowledge, constitute the material object of metaphysics. It can offer judgments on anything.

AC: Coming away from a reading of St Thomas Aquinas,

149

Leibniz, Guénon, or Schuon, these are even authoritative judgments.

BB: They have the form of it, but the authority is neither that of St Thomas Aquinas, Leibniz, Guénon, or Schuon; it is, rather, that given by the point of view of the absolute, or more precisely of a *personal,* point of view, but one that embraces both the absolute and the relative. There is both the intellect common to every human being *and* the metaphysician who experiences it. We must not forget that "it is not the intellect that knows, but man." (Aristotle) Man sees through the intellect, but it is with his reason that he is able to convey what he sees. The intellect allows him to contemplate, beyond concepts, the essences of all things, because they agree to give themselves to him. To speak about it, one has, on the one hand, only poetry, paradoxes, even oxymorons; and on the other, conceptual language. When it comes to speaking about it, there is both what any metaphysical mind will be able to understand and what comes from the particular man: his own discourse, his own history, his own idiosyncrasies. The mirror that is the intelligence, necessarily has its dark side (Borella).

AC: Hence this possibility of criticizing any metaphysical discourse or any metaphysician who holds it, without prejudice to either the inexpressible matters contemplated or the metaphysical person who intends to share that experience.

BB: Exactly. Dust does not affect light. And that applies to the metaphysics I am trying to share. It is even fortunate that any metaphysical discourse can be criticized. Let there be no mistake about authority.

AC: Ultimately, the only authority, then, is God.

Metaphysics as theology

BB: It is God, in fact, and by whatever name we give him: "the cause before the cause" (Archaenetus), the "Universal Principle" (Philolaus), the "First Cause" or the "first unmoved Mover" (Aristotle), the "One-Good" (Plato, Plotinus), or, more recently, the "First Principle" or the "Infinite" (Descartes), the "ultimate reason of things" (Leibniz), the Absolute, All-Possibility, Non-Being (Guénon), Beyond-Being (Schuon), Ultimate Reality (Chenique), etc.

AC: This great variation in vocabulary is certainly not insignificant, but "God" will do just fine.

BB: Absolutely. And it is significant that these latest metaphysicians have unambiguously declared their affiliations. They are, without exception, Christians, Muslims, and a Hindu.

AC: But in terms of religion, what about the Greek metaphysicians, five hundred years before Jesus Christ?

BB: It is certainly religion that opens the mind to an awareness of the supernatural, to what stands beyond man, to the fact that things are not entirely there and have their cause in a beyond, etc. It is also from Christianity that the notion of religion was born and that the religions of the earth were identified as such (Borella). Prior to that time, one spoke in terms of sacred societies. This is obvious, as for example when we read about the "Chosen People" of Israel in the Old Testament; or in India, where we encounter *shruti* (revealed cognizance) in a *Upanishad* that dates to around 800 BC.

Among the Greeks, it suffices to read Parmenides or Heraclitus to discover a sacred regime of knowledge. It will even be, after the crisis of the Sophists, Plato's entire effort to aim at rediscovering this sacred regime of pure knowledge. For him, it is the dialectic of concepts that allows them to be led back to their *Idea*, to their metaphysical principle (Borella).

AC: Metaphysics is therefore a believing in God!

BB: By compulsion, so to speak. One cannot experience the transcendent and deny God, except by falling into the contradictions of the philosophers of the death of God. Moreover, whatever the name given, once "experienced," belief in the reality behind the name is established.

AC: And can you repeat what it is to believe?

BB: To go to the end of what it is to believe, I would say that it is to die in advance.

To believe is to die in advance

AC: But isn't there a kind of belief that comes from the symbolic, affirmative, and negative theologies you spoke of in a previous interview?

BB: Of course, there is almost always a dogmatic belief...

AC: Dogmatic?

BB: I am thinking of Christian dogma itself, which is the sum-total of the most transparent possible formulations of the Christian mysteries: one God in three persons, Christ as true man and true God, etc. Let us say, more generally, that there are conceptual beliefs: for example, Allahu akbar ("God is Great") in Islam, and "nothing but the Self exists" in Hinduism, as well as the doctrines of the creation of the world, of the end of time, human perspectives on after-death states, the notions of charity (Christianity) or compassion (Buddhism, Islam), etc.

AC: That's a whole lot of information!

BB: We should speak rather of knowledge or beliefs, because, with God, his existence is the only obvious thing; all the rest, ultimately, is unspeakable, if not unknowable. In other words, in the very depths of believing (as we said in the interview on the metaphysics of believing) there is almost nothing left. As we have spoken about at length, this is primarily because you renounce any knowledge, you abandon all concepts, especially those concepts which create idols of God (St Gregory of Nyssa), and "there are in the world more 'idols than realities'" (Nietzsche).

AC: This abandonment of concepts is the gnostic moment of mystical theology, after all knowledge about God is repudiated.

BB: Yes, but only if we chance upon this gnostic moment, or rather if we benefit from this grace. We neither provoke nor force the epiphany of the Spirit. It is therefore not appropriate to concern oneself with gnosis. It is part of the necessary renunciations. Such renunciation is recommended everywhere: in Christianity, Judaism, Islam, Taoism:

> Blessed are those intelligences who know how to close their eyes. (St Dionysius the Areopagite)

> Because all the intelligence that we have of them remains so unequal in the sense of these mysteries in themselves and in God that we can take it for nothing. (Meister Eckhart)

> God is ungraspable:
> God is a sheer Nothing, no *here*, no *today*
> Touches Him ever—

The more you reach out, the more He slips away. (Angelus Silesius, *Cherubinic Wanderer* I, 25)

Intelligence, discrimination and analysis cannot find the Dao, only *xiangwang* (the absence of form and intention) can succeed. (Zhuangzi)

If knowledge does not take you away from yourself, then ignorance will be a hundred times better than that knowledge. (Shams-ed-Din Tabrizi)

"What" do you understand? "What" were you looking for? For everything is as mysterious as before. (*Zohar*, I, 1b)

AC: What then remains after these renunciations?

BB: There still remains an "I" that renounces; this "I" still has to be renounced:

Individuality must be consumed. (Ramana Maharshi)

You have to die to yourself, but far beyond a simple abnegation. One must be totally hopeless, emptied of the present and future worlds (Ibrahim ben Adham), naked, empty, impersonal (*anatta*), annihilated. The self must be allowed to annihilate itself (Kitaro Nishida), to become emptiness (*sunyata*), to die out (al-fan'a)...

God is not found by the soul, as long as it has not been reduced to nothing... Whoever wants to come to God must come with nothing. (Meister Eckhart)

Self-annihilation:
Only the annihilated state lifts you above yourself;

154

the most annihilated is also the most divine. (Angelus Silesius, *Cherubinic Wanderer* II, 140)

To become Nothing is to become God:
Nothing becomes what already is;
If you do not anticipate becoming naught,
You will never be born of eternal Light. (Angelus Silesius, *Cherubinic Wanderer,* VI, 130)

What remains, then, is an ontological *speck:* a pure sallying forth, a residuum of being, *a zest for being perfumed with hope*, a pure belief.

Appendix I

Analogy of the divided line
Plato, *Republic*, VI and VII

One-Good beyond everything

	Order of being	Order of knowing	
REGION OF THE INTELLIGIBLE	*Ideas*	intuitive cognizance by dialectic ascent of the *intellect* (*noesis*)	SCIENCE
	concepts (*mathematics*)	hypothetico-deductive knowledge thru *discursive reason* (*dianoia*)	
REGION OF THE SENSIBLE	*realities* natural & fabricated	knowledge by *faith in experience* (*pistis*)	OPINION
	images and reflections	knowledge by *imagination* and conjecture (*eikasia*)	

Order of being   *Order of knowing*

Appendix II

The Two-Step "Cure"

Tradition	First Step *Centering in the horizon of amplitude*	Second Step *Exaltation through the vertical axis*
Sufism	*al-fana* (extinction)	*fana' al-fanai* extinction of extinction
Hinduism	*nirvana* (*nivritti*) (extinction, return)	*parinirvana* (*parinivritti*) total extinction
Judaism	*Sch'mittah* Presence of God	*Yobel* Supreme Illumination and Identity
Taoism	*tchenn-jen* (true man)	*cheun-jen* (transcendent man)
Buddhism (*Hinayana*)	*Sopadhishesanirvana* (state of *Arhat*: liberated)	*Nirupadhishesanirvana* complete liberation
Buddhism (*Mahayana*)	*Bodhi* (skt.); *satori* (jap.) (awakening)	*Pratishitanirvana* (realization of the state of Buddha)
Christianity	Illuminated The New Man of Redemption Becoming Virgin	Consummated in charity The Perfect Man of the Parousia and Pleroma Giving birth to Christ by the Father's Will
	Immanence	*Transcendence*

Appendix III

Some Texts about Believing

"Such is my prayer. For you, dear Timothy, exercise yourself unceasingly in mystical contemplations, abandon sensations, renounce intellectual operations, reject all that belongs to the sensible and the intelligible, strip yourself completely of non-being and of being, and so elevate yourself, as far as you can, until you unite in ignorance with Him who is beyond all essence and all knowledge. For it is by laying aside everything and yourself, in an irresistible and perfect way, that you will rise in pure ecstasy to the tenebrous ray of the divine Super-Essence, having abandoned everything and stripped yourself of everything." (St Dionysius the Areopagite, *Mystical Theology*, chap. I, §1)

"When I return to God, if I do not remain there, my breakthrough will be far nobler than my outflowing. I alone bring all creatures out of their reason into my reason, so that they are one with me. When I enter the ground, the bottom, the river and fount of the Godhead, none will ask me whence I came or where I have been. No one missed me, for there God *unbecomes*. Whoever has understood this sermon, good luck to him. If no one had been here I should have had to preach it to this offertory box. There are some poor people who will go back home and say, 'I shall settle down and eat my bread and serve God.' By the eternal truth I declare that these people will remain in error, and will never be able to strive for and win what those oth-

ers achieve who follow God in poverty and exile. Amen."
(Meister Eckhart, Sermon 56, ed. O'C Walshe, 294)

"A man should be so poor that he neither is nor has any
place for God to work in... Therefore I pray to God to
make me free of God, for my essential being is above God,
taking God as the origin of creatures. For in that essence of
God in which God is above being and distinction, there I
was myself and knew myself so as to make this man. Therefore I am my own cause according to my essence, which is
eternal, and not according to my becoming, which is temporal.

"Therefore I am unborn, and according to my unborn
mode I can never die. According to my unborn mode I
have eternally been, am now, and shall eternally remain.
That which I am by virtue of birth must die and perish, for
it is mortal, and so must perish with time. In my birth all
things were born, and I was the cause of myself and all
things: and if I had so willed it, I would not have been, and
all things would not have been. If I were not, God would
not be either. I am the cause of God's being God: if I were
not, then God would not be God...

"But in my breaking-through, where I stand free of my
own will, of God's will, of all His works, and of God himself, *then* I am above all creatures and am neither God nor
creature, but I am that which I was and shall remain for
evermore. There I shall receive an imprint that will raise me
above all the angels. By this imprint I shall gain such wealth
that I shall not be content with God inasmuch as He is
God, or with all His divine works: for this breaking-
through guarantees to me that I and God are one. *Then* I
am what I was, then I neither wax nor wane, for then I am

an unmoved cause that moves all things. Here, God finds no place *in* man, for man by his poverty wins for himself what he has eternally been and shall eternally remain. Here, God is one with the spirit, and that is the strictest poverty one can find.

"If anyone cannot understand this sermon, he need not worry. For so long as a man is not equal to this truth, he cannot understand my words, for this is a naked truth which has come direct from the heart of God.

"That we may so live as to experience it eternally, may God help us. Amen." (Meister Eckhart, Sermon 87; O'C. Walshe, 424–425)

"Then there remains in our intellect only this: it is, and nothing more. But, in the end, this very being, in the form in which it is found in creatures, we deny it for Him, and then [our intellect] remains in a kind of night of ignorance which unites us to God in the most perfect way, insofar as it appertains to this life." (St Thomas Aquinas, *Commentaries on the Book of Sentences* L. I, dist. VIII, art. 1, rep. 4)

"This immovable detachment brings a man into the greatest likeness to God. For the reason why God is God is because of His immovable detachment, and from this detachment He has His purity, His simplicity, and His immutability... This likeness must occur through grace, for grace draws man away from all temporal things and purges him of all that is transient." (Meister Eckhart, "On Detachment"; O'C. Walshe, 569)

"Divine Life is indeed the pattern for man, made in the image of God. This life is conceived in man by Grace, which is the perfect equivalence, in Charity, between total Poverty and absolute Wealth: ideal Love (Charity) gives everything (Wealth) and expects nothing (Poverty). 'Expect nothing'!—because hope is not hope, because hope for an unspeakable Good is not the hope for an imaginable good. 'Though he slay me, yet will I trust in him,' said Job (13:15). Because it is absolute trust in the Love of God, by grace, which allows total abandonment. Because it is 'the Spirit himself [who] prays for us with ineffable groanings' (Rom. 8:26)." (Bérard, *Introduction to a Metaphysics of Christian Mysteries*)

"For everything that is understood and sensed is nothing else but the apparition of what is not apparent, the manifestation of the hidden, the affirmation of the negated, the comprehension of the incomprehensible, the utterance of the unutterable, the access to the inaccessible, the understanding of the unintelligible, the body of the bodiless, the essence of the superessential, the form of the formless, the measure of the measureless, the number of the unnumbered, the weight of the weightless, the materialization of the spiritual, the visibility of the invisible, the place of that which is in no place, the time of the timeless, the definition of the infinite, the circumscription of the uncircumscribed…" (John the Scot, *Periphyseon* 3, 633AB)

"The only purpose of hermeneutics (i.e., interpretation or search for meaning) is thus to lead us where knowledge becomes useless, for there knowledge becomes being, where knowledge becomes impossible and therefore useless. And it is the very nature of a path that its end is no longer the path itself (by definition).

"There, our ontological speck is totally stripped of any relative truth, of any personal journey, of any life of its own: it is the Virgin!

"There, this ontological speck, this virgin creature, can espouse the only Truth, the only Way, and the true Life that is Christ!

"This absolute Truth and this Eternal Life are this unique Way that leads to the Father by the total Gift of the Son in the Spirit. There begins the motionless whirlwind of the absolute and reciprocal Gifts of the three Persons, who 'contain each other mutually' (St John Damascene): this is the Trinity!" (Bérard, *Introduction to a Metaphysics of Christian Mysteries*)

From the Same Author
(Bruno Bérard)

Works

Introduction à une métaphysique des mystères chrétiens (*en regard des traditions bouddhique, hindoue, islamique, judaïque et taoïste*), L'Harmattan, 2005, *imprimatur* (Paris) n° 20 (janv. 2003).

Jean Borella: la Révolution métaphysique après Galilée, Kant, Marx, Freud, Derrida, L'Harmattan, 2006, apostille de Jean Borella.

Introduction à la métaphysique. Les trois songes, préface de M. Cazenave, L'Harmattan, 2009.

Métaphysique du paradoxe, t. 1. *Paradoxes et limites du savoir, t.* 2. *La Connaissance paradoxale, L'Harmattan,* 2019.

Lacuria, un philosophe et théologien occultisant au XIXᵉ s., t. 1 & 2, ART édition, 2020.

Métaphysique du sexe, L'Harmattan, 2022.

—*La démocratie du futur, le partage du pouvoir,* L'Harmattan, 2022.

Conversations avec ChatGPT, Postface de Johannes Hoff, L'Harmattan, 2024.

—with Aldo La Fata and an Orthodox monk, *Théologie pour tous,* L'Harmattan, 2024.

—with Jean Borella, *Métaphysique des contes de fées,* L'Harmattan, 2011.

—in English

A Metaphysics of the Christian Mystery. Introduction to Jean Borella's Work, ed. John Champoux, Tacoma (WA): Angelico Press, 2018.

From the Same Author

—in Italian

Introduzione a una metafisica cristiana, Roma: Simmetria, 2021.

—with Annie Cideron, *Sui sentieri della metafisica, Intervista a Bruno Bérard,* Roma: Simmetria, 2024.

—with Aldo La Fata, *Che cosè l'ésoterisme, Tra verità e contraffazioni,* Cheti: Solfanelli, 2024.

Collective Works (Dir.)

Qu'est-ce que la métaphysique?, L'Harmattan, 2010.

Métaphysique et psychanalyse, L'Harmattan, 2013.

Physique et métaphysique, L'Harmattan, 2018.

—in English

Rediscovering the Integral Cosmos: Physics, Metaphysics, and Vertical Causality, Bruno Bérard (introduction), Jean Borella, Wolfgang Smith, Angelico Press, 2018.

Forewords

Qu'est-ce que la métaphysique? collectif, L'Harmattan, 2010.

Jean Biès, *Le soleil se lève à minuit. Initiation aux sagesses du quotidien,* L'Harmattan, 2011.

Métaphysique et psychanalyse, collectif, L'Harmattan, 2013.

Physique et métaphysique, collectif, L'Harmattan, 2018.

—in English

Jean Borella, Wolfgang Smith, *Rediscovering the Integral Cosmos: Physics, Metaphysics, and Vertical Causality,* Angelico Press, 2018.

Wolfgang Smith, *The Vertical Ascent, from Particles to the Tripartite Universe and Beyond,* Angelico Press, 2020.

Articles and Conferences (extract)

"Jean Borella: distinguer entre intelligence et raison," in *Au commencement est le cœur*, Alain Santacreu (ed.), L'Harmattan, 2010.

"René Guénon, l'ésotérisme et le christianisme," in *Au commencement est le cœur*, Alain Santacreu (ed.), L'Harmattan, 2010.

"Faut-il être intelligent pour être sauvé?" site de Contrelittérature, 2010. 2.

"Retour vers une métaphysique du Beau," *Du religieux dans l'art*, Alain Santacreu (ed.), L'Harmattan, 2012.

"Un prêtre indépendant au XIXᵉ siècle: l'abbé Lacuria (1806–1890)," *Politica Hermetica* n° 30, 2017 (pp. 159 *sq*).

Conférence *Politica Hermetica*: "Un prêtre indépendant au XIXᵉ siècle, l'abbé Lacuria," 10 avril 2015, couvent de l'Annonciation, Paris.

"Les Jardins Philosophiques #1: Bruno Bérard, https://www.you tube.com/watch?v=j6IHQJAm8q4, mars 2020.

—in English

"*Unmasking 'AI'*," site 'of *Philos-Sophia.org*, 22 February 2018.

—in Italian

"*La metafisica come anti-dogmatismo e non-sistema*," trans. Aldo La Fata, *Il Corriere Metapolitico*, year three, no. 9, Dec. 2019.

"*Chrono-Sophia, Riflessioni sulla fine dei tempi*," trad. Aldo La Fata, *Il Corriere Metapolitico*, year four, no. 10, April 2020.

"*La Guarigione in due tempi*," trans. Aldo La Fata, *Il Corriere Metapolitico*, year five, no. 13, April 2021.

"*L'ologramma cristologico o il Cristo olagrammatico*," trans. Aldo La Fata, *Il Corriere Metapolitico*, year five, no. 14, September 2021.

Index of Names

A

Adam · 31, 128
Adham, Ibrahim ben · 154
Aggrawal, Anil · 125
Anselm (St) · 48, 50–51, 104, 119
Aquinas, Thomas (St) · 27, 32–33, 36–38, 43–44, 46, 50, 63, 76, 91, 94, 99–103, 123, 134, 140, 149
Arabi, Ibn · 63, 89, 123, 128
Archaenetus · 151
Aristotle · 5–7, 11, 13, 15–16, 19, 26–28, 31–36, 38–39, 43–44, 48–49, 58, 63, 94–95, 97–101, 106, 118, 129, 132–33, 151
Athanasius (St) · 142
Aubenque, Pierre · 16, 28, 34
Augustine (St) · 27, 32, 44, 102, 104, 142, 147
Averroes · 63, 100
Avicenna · 63, 100

B

Baden-Powell, Robert · 72
Bastaire, Jean · 125
Bazin, Hervé · 115
Behe, Michael J. · 44
Benedict XVI (pope) · 124
Benzine, Rachid · 92
Bergson, Henri · 63, 95
Bernard of Clairvaux · 68
Biale, David · 125
Binet, Alfred · 148
Blanke, Olaf · 47
Blondel, Maurice · 63, 95

Böhme, Jakob · 128
Bonaventure (St) · 36–37, 54, 63, 102, 141
Borella, Jean · 6, 12, 15–17, 27–30, 34, 38–42, 45, 48–52, 67, 72, 75, 77, 80–86, 91–92, 97, 99–101, 109–11, 116–22, 128–29, 135–36, 141, 143–44, 146–47, 150–52
Borg, Jacqueline · 47
Bossuet, Jacques-Bénigne · 44, 95
Brach, Jean-Pierre · 86
Brothers of Sincerity · 54
Bultmann, Rudolf · 122
Burckhardt, Titus · 41, 108
Buren, John van · 101

C

Carnap, Rudolf · 46, 137
Carrère, Emmanuel · 21
Carter, Brandon · 44
Chanterelle (Lanza del Vasto's wife) · 74
Chenique, François · 9, 37, 41, 71–72, 75, 77–78, 80–81, 84, 96–97, 102, 135, 145, 151
Christ · 13, 33, 81–82, 143–45, 151–52, 163
Clarke, Samuel · 44
Clauberg, Johann · 13
Clement of Alexandria · 53–54
Comte-Sponville, André · 24
Coomaraswamy, Ananda · 41, 108
Craig, William L. · 43, 45

Cusa, Nicholas of · 54, 108, 141
Cyrulnik, Boris · 64

D
Damascene, John (St) · 163
Darwin, Charles · 23
Dawkins, Richard · 23
Dembski, William · 44
Derrida, Jacques · 110, 137,
    147–49
Descartes, René · 48–49, 51, 63,
    89, 95, 103–4, 109, 119, 123,
    147, 151
DeWitt, Bryce · 138
Dilthey, Wilhelm · 8
Diner, Simon · 137
Dionysius the Areopagite (St) ·
    32–33, 38, 78–79, 121, 123,
    119, 140, 153, 159
Dogen · 63
Dubost, Michel (Mgr) · 81
Duméry, Henry · 36
Duns Scotus · 32

E
Eckhart, Meister · 32–33, 63,
    78–79, 103, 118, 123, 131, 140,
    145, 153–54, 160–61
Einstein, Albert · 137
Ellul, Jacques · 115
Epley, Nicholas · 47
Espagnat, Bernard d' · 138
Evdokimov, Paul · 125
Eve · 31, 128
Evola, Julius · 15, 88–89, 124

F
Faivre, Antoine · 54
Farabi, Al- · 62
Ferry, Luc · 23, 25
Feuerbach, Ludwig · 47, 109

Foucault, Michel · 149
Freud, Sigmund · 25, 47, 109
Frossard, André · 115

G
Galileo (di Vincenzo Bonaiuti
    de' Galilei) · 109
Gandhi, Mohandas Karam-
    chand · 74
Gauchet, Marcel · 22–23
George, James · 32
Gérard de Nerval (Gérard La-
    brunie, dit) · 22
Gil, Fernando · 116
Gilson, Etienne · 36, 39, 102
Gödel, Kurt · 10
Goettmann, Alphonse and
    Rachel · 125
Gouhier, Henri · 37
Gregory of Nyssa (St) · 153
Guénon, René · 13, 15, 17, 30–
    33, 39, 41, 59, 63, 78, 105–11,
    123, 139, 150–51
Guitton, Jean · 115

H
Hamilton, William · 101
Hawking, Stephen · 23, 46
Hegel, Georg Wilhelm
    Friedrich · 22
Heidegger, Martin · 15–16, 39,
    41–42, 63, 79, 111, 137
Heine, Christian Johann
    Heinrich · 22
Heraclitus · 14, 89, 151
Hermes Trismegistus · 53
Hesychius of Miletus · 6

I
Idel, Moshe · 125
Inwagen, Peter van · 46

J
Jeans, James · 136
John the Scot · 54, 162

K
Kant, Immanuel · 15, 21–22, 33,
 39, 41, 45–46, 48–51, 89, 95,
 100–1, 110–11, 117, 125, 137,
 147–49
Kindi, al- · 43
Kouchner, Bernard · 115
Krishnamurti · 38
Kukai · 63

L
La Fata, Aldo · 86
Lachièze-Rey, Marc · 137
Landauer, Rolf · 132
Lanza del Vasto · 12, 72, 74, 91
Lao Tzu · 63
Laplace, Pierre Simon · 12, 46
Laurant, Jean-Pierre · 31, 58, 86
Leibniz, Gottfried Wilhelm ·
 21, 39, 43–44, 47–48, 51, 63,
 89, 103–5, 129, 150–51

M
Maharshi, Ramana · 154
Malebranche, Nicolas · 121
Mlodinow, Leonard · 23
Mokdad, Mensia Arfa · 128
Monod, Jacques · 149
Montaigne, Michel de · 117, 123
Muhammad, Prophet · 29

N
Nagarjuna · 63
Napoleon · 12
Nédoncelle, Maurice · 45
Newman, John Henry (St) · 47
Newton, Isaac · 45

Nicolaus of Damascus · 5
Nietzsche, Friedrich · 19–20,
 25, 89, 109, 153
Nishida, Kitaro · 63, 154
Nouwen, Henri · 78

O
Onfrey, Michel · 23
Origen · 30, 53–54

P
Paley, William · 44
Pamphile · 7, 20, 72, 77, 84
Parmenides · 14–15, 151
Pascal, Blaise · 20, 25, 68, 123
Paul (St) · 122
Persinger, Michael · 47
Philolaus · 151
Planck, Max · 92, 136–37
Plato · 6, 14–15, 17–19, 27–28,
 31–39, 42–44, 48–49, 52–53,
 58, 63, 65–67, 79, 88–89, 92,
 94–95, 97–99, 103, 106, 117–
 18, 121–22, 125, 133, 136, 138,
 140, 143, 151
Plotinus · 63, 151
Popper, Karl · 10

Q
Quine, Willard Van Orman ·
 42

R
Ramakrishna · 30
Ricœur, Paul · 109
Rolland, Romain · 25
Russell, Bertrand · 46

S
Sankara/Shankara · 63, 107, 123
Schaya, Leo · 30, 41, 108, 134

Schopenhauer, Arthur · 48, 64, 89, 95, 125
Schrödinger, Erwin · 87
Schuon, Frithjof · 13, 16, 29–30, 32, 39, 41, 63, 96, 106–8, 110–11, 125, 140, 150–51
Senghor, Léopold Sédar · 115
Sheldrake, Rupert · 44
Sherrard, Philip Owen Arnould · 125
Silesius, Angelus (Johannes Scheffler) · 32, 123, 154–55
Simon, Théodore · 148
Smith, Wolfgang · 23, 44, 84, 131
Socrates · 117
Spinoza, Baruch · 89
Stéphane (Fr) · 78, 80–81, 109
Swedenborg, Emmanuel · 128

T
Tabrizi, Shams-ed-Din · 154
Thérèse of Lisieux (St) · 145

V
Vahanian, Gabriel · 101
Verlinde, Joseph-Marie · 22, 25
Verne, Jules · 142
Voltaire (François-Marie Arouet) · 24, 43, 105

W
Weber, Max · 22
Weil, Simone · 65
Weininger, Otto · 126
Wittgenstein, Ludwig · 39

Z
Zhuangzi · 154
Zolli, Israel · 115

www.ingramcontent.com/pod-product-compliance
Lightning Source LLC
Chambersburg PA
CBHW022022090426
42739CB00006BA/249